THE ALPS

OTTO SIEGNER

THE ALPS

CHARLES SCRIBNER'S SONS, NEW YORK

With an Introduction by
Dr. Franz Grassler

„Alpen, Alpen, unvergeßlich seid
Meinem Herzen ihr in allen Tagen"
Nikolaus Lenau, 1802—1850

"The playground of Europe"
Titel eines Bergbuches von
Leslie Stephen, 1871

Die Seelenheimat des Dichters — der Spielplatz des sportlich denkenden Bergsteigers; zwischen diesen beiden Polen finden wir viele Möglichkeiten, die Alpen zu betrachten:

Dem Geographen, Geologen, Mineralogen, Glaziologen und vielen anderen Wissenschaftlern geben sie seit uralten Zeiten Gelegenheit zu forschen, einzuteilen, Theorien (und natürlich Gegentheorien) aufzustellen und Bücher zu schreiben.

Die wirtschaftliche Bedeutung der Alpen lag früher in ihrem Reichtum an Erzen, Salz, Holz; heute sind sie die Ferienlandschaft Europas. Der Fremdenverkehr ist für die Alpenländer zum bestimmenden Faktor geworden; seine Bedeutung wurde annähernd verdoppelt durch die Verbreitung des Skilaufs.

Dem Verkehr waren die Alpen früher das größte Hindernis innerhalb des Kontinents. Die Techniker haben gelernt, sie seit Römerzeiten durch Paßstraßen, seit der Mitte des 19. Jahrhunderts durch Eisenbahnen zu überwinden; immer länger wurden die Tunnels, und den letzten Schrei stellt die „Überseilung" ganzer Gebirgsmassive mit Bergbahnen dar.

Hirten und Jäger waren wohl die ersten Menschen, die in die Hochregionen der Alpen eindrangen, doch die Einheimischen blieben nicht unter sich. Sie wurden übertroffen durch Intellektuelle aus den Städten, die zunächst als Forscher kamen — oder sich als solche ausgaben, wenn sie nur neugierig waren; ein neues Verhältnis zur Natur legitimierte schließlich die Neugier und ließ den Alpinismus zur Massenbewegung werden.

Eine Massenbewegung, die nicht nur in den Alpenländern zu eigenen Organisationen führte. Daß der erste Alpenverein im alpenfernen London (Alpine Club, 1857) entstand, war kein Zufall, denn die planmäßige Erschließung der Alpen — insbesondere der Westalpen — war in erster Linie englischen Alpinisten (wenn auch mit einheimischen Führern) zu verdanken. Die Bergsteiger der Alpenländer zogen ohne Eile nach: 1862 Österreichischer Alpenverein (ÖAV), 1863 Schweizer Alpenclub (SAC) und Club Alpino Italiano (CAI), 1869 Deutscher Alpenverein (DAV) und 1874 Club Alpin Français (CAF); von 1874 bis 1945 waren DAV und ÖAV im Deutschen und Österreichischen Alpenverein (DÖAV) vereint. Bergsteigerverbände gibt es heute in beinahe allen Ländern der Erde — und seien sie noch so flach; sie nennen sich vielfach „Alpenklub" auch fern der Alpen (z. B. in Neuseeland, Japan und den USA). Da gleichgesinnte Vereine nach einem Dachverband streben, fanden sich die Bergsteigerorganisationen aus Europa und aus Übersee, aus (politisch gesehen) Ost und West zur Union Internationale des Associations d'Alpinisme zusammen.

Diese Massenbewegung befruchtete wiederum manche Sparten der Kunst; sie brachte ein umfangreiches alpines Schrifttum und eine alpine Malerei hervor. Die größte Fachbibliothek der Erde, die Alpenvereinsbücherei in München, hatte ca. 60000 Titel, als sie 1943 größtenteils zerstört wurde; sie verfügt heute wieder über ca. 24000 Titel und 2000 Karten, und sie sammelt etwa 250 einschlägige Zeitschriften.

*

„Das Hochgebirge der Alpen giebt Mittel-Europa seine eigenthümliche, erhabene Gestaltung. Sein Einfluß erstreckt sich weit nach allen Seiten in den Welttheil hinein ... Die Alpen erkälten zwar Mittel-Europa um ein

Beträchtliches, aber sie entschädigen dafür reichlich durch die erhabene Pracht ihrer Formen, durch die reiche Bewässerung, welche die umliegenden Länder tränkt, und durch das eigenthümliche Colorit der Frische und Schönheit, welches ihnen selbst eigen ist und welches sie um sich verbreiten. Die Alpen sind die Krone von Europa, die in ihren ewigen Firnen schimmert."

Mit diesen poetischen Worten beginnt der preußische Hauptmann und Geograf H. Beitzke sein 902 Seiten starkes Werk „Die Alpen" (Colberg, 1843). Nüchtern sagt das Lexikon: „Alpen, das höchste Gebirge Europas; es erstreckt sich zwischen 43½° und 48° n. Br. und 5° und 16½° ö. L. In einem gegen W konvex und nach O langhin geschwungenen Bogen zieht es vom Golf von Genua bis Wien und zur Karstpforte. Am Paß von Altare (459 m) ist die Grenze zum Apennin anzusetzen … In dieser Umrahmung sind sie etwa 1300 km lang, 150 bis 250 km breit … Die Alpen bedecken auf der Karte eine Fläche von 220000 qkm" (Brockhaus Enzyklopädie 1967 ff.).

Es dauerte Jahrhunderte, bis dieses Wissen über die Alpen abschließend geklärt war. Die Geographen des Altertums kannten die wahre Ausdehnung des Alpenbogens nicht, und noch 1574 schrieb der Schweizer Josias Simler in „De alpibus commentarius", dem ersten umfassenden Alpenbuch überhaupt: „Wir folgen der Ansicht jener alten Autoren, die sagen: Die eigentlichen Alpen sind jenes Gebirge, das Italien begrenzt". Nebenbei gesagt, das XIV. Kapitel dieses Werkes über „Schwierigkeiten und Gefahren der Reisewege in den Alpen und wie man sie bewältigt" stellt das erste Lehrbuch des Bergsteigens dar.

Soviel wir heute auch über die Alpen wissen mögen, über ihre Einteilung besteht noch keine volle Einigkeit. Gegenüber einer früher einmal vorgeschlagenen Dreiteilung in Französisch-italienische Alpen, Schweizer oder Mittelalpen und Ostalpen hat sich die Zweiteilung in West- und Ostalpen allgemein durchgesetzt. Daß dafür die Grenze am Splügenpaß liegt (Rhein–Hinterrhein–Splügen–Liro–Mera–Comer See), ist unter den Wissenschaftlern nicht mehr sonderlich umstritten, aber sie geht manchem

alpinen Schriftsteller gegen das Gefühl, denn sie „empfinden" Bernina und Bergell „nach ihrem deutlich erkennbaren westalpinen Landschaftscharakter als Bestandteil der Westalpen" (K. Lukan, „Das große Ostalpenbuch", 1969). Die häufig anzutreffenden Gefühls-Geographen überlegen aber nicht, daß sie mit einer willkürlichen Verschiebung der Grenzlinie nach Osten — etwa in die Nähe der Schweizer Landesgrenze — keine natürliche Grenze mehr finden und daß sie (von Bernina und Bergell abgesehen) fünf Gebirgsgruppen ohne westalpinen Charakter (Plessur-, Oberhalbstein-, Albula-, Livigno- und Bergamasker Alpen) den Westalpen zuschlagen.

Wenn ich im folgenden versuche, gewissermaßen in einem Flug über die Alpen vom Mittelmeer bis zur Donau die wichtigsten Gebirgsgruppen, die interessantesten Berge, die bedeutendsten Orte, die großen Verkehrswege und herausstechende Ereignisse der alpinen Geschichte zu nennen, wird die Systematik der Alpeneinteilung nur eine Art Leitfaden sein; alle Gruppen der Alpen einzeln zu würdigen ginge weit über den Sinn dieser Einführung zu einem Bildwerk über die Alpen hinaus. Ich bitte es mir auch nachzusehen, daß ich auf Pflichtübungen auf dem Gebiet der Geologie und ähnlicher (als Zeichen der Allgemeinbildung des Autors üblicherweise angesprochener) Wissenschaften verzichte.

Westalpen

Über den Palmenpromenaden, den Spielkasinos und den Fleischmärkten der Riviera stehen die Gipfel der *Ligurischen* und der *Meer- oder See-Alpen*, die in der Punta Argentera immerhin schon zur Höhe von 3297 m aufsteigen. Hier liegen auch die südlichsten Wintersportplätze Frankreichs, Auron und Valberg; ihre Entfernung von Nizza (ca. 90 km) erlaubt es, im Frühling an einem Tag über die Schneepisten zu jagen und an der Côte d'Azur Wasserskilauf zu betreiben.

Als Bergland ohne Hochgebirgscharakter schließen sich im Westen die *Provençalischen Kalkalpen* an. Hier finden wir die Gorges du Verdon, die gewaltigste Schlucht Europas, und als Aussichtspunkt ersten Ranges den Mont Ventoux (1912 m). An ihm begann die Geschichte des Bergsteigens in den Alpen. Der Dichter Francesco Petrarca bestieg ihn mit seinem Bruder Gerhard am 26. April 1336; er schrieb an Kardinal Colonna: „Den höchsten Berg unserer Gegend, der nicht unverdienterweise der windige genannt wird, habe ich gestern bestiegen, lediglich aus Verlangen, die namhafte Höhe des Ortes kennenzulernen." Er gibt unumwunden preis, daß ihn letztlich jene Leidenschaft getrieben hat, die Ursprung aller Taten in der alpinen Geschichte war: „Jener Berg, weit und breit sichtbar, stand mir fast allezeit vor Augen, allmählich ward mein Verlangen ungestüm."

Als gewaltiger Block, in dem (von Süden her gesehen) erstmals die Viertausend-Meter-Grenze überschritten wird, folgen im Norden den See- und Provence-Alpen die Cottischen und die Dauphiné-Alpen. Turin im Osten und Grenoble im Westen sind die Tore in diese beiden bedeutenden Gebirgsgruppen. Der Querverbindung zwischen Italien und Frankreich dient die Eisenbahnlinie, die nach dem Mont Cenis benannt ist, tatsächlich aber in einem 12 km langen Tunnel den Col de Fréjus unterfährt; die Kraftwagen rollen über den Col du Mont Cenis (2084 m; zwischen Susa und Lanslebourg) oder über den Col de Montgenèvre (zwischen Susa und Briançon). Paßstraßenspezialisten finden einen ganzen Autoführer voll interessanter Pässe in den französischen Alpen, wenn sie diese in der Längsrichtung befahren. Allein die großartige „Route des Alpes" quert zwischen Thonon am Genfer See und Nizza zehn Pässe, von denen sechs höher als 2000 m (höchster: Col de l'Iseran, 2770 m) liegen; weiter westlich verbindet die „Route Napoléon" Grenoble mit Cannes.

In den nach einem sagenhaften König Cottius benannten *Cottischen Alpen* sind ein Berg und ein Ort weithin bekannt: der Monte Viso und Sestriere. Am Fuße des 3843 m hohen Monte Viso, des „isoliertesten, seine Umgebung am gewaltigsten beherrschenden Gipfels des ganzen Alpensystems" (Umlauft) entspringt der Po. Wenn auch seine Erstbesteigung 1861 Engländern mit französi-

schen Führern gelang, ist er doch der Berg der Italiener; auf seinem Gipfel beschlossen 1863 der bergbegeisterte Minister Quintino Sella und seine Freunde die Gründung eines italienischen Alpenklubs. Ab 1931 entstand als erster auf dem Reißbrett konstruierter Wintersportplatz auf Veranlassung des Chefs der FIAT-Werke Senator Agnelli das durch seine Turmhotels berühmt gewordene Sestriere.

Im Blickfeld der Pisten von Sestriere liegen im Westen die hohen Berge der *Dauphiné-Alpen*. Auch hier gibt es „vollmechanisierte Skiparadiese" wie etwa Alpe d'Huez, Les deux Alpes und Chamrousse, doch der Name Dauphiné hat vor allem bei den Bergsteigern höchsten Klang; ihr Mekka ist das Dörfchen La Grave unter dem Col du Lautaret oder aber die wenigen Häuser des weltabgeschiedenen La Bérarde im Vénéontal, zwischen denen sich das gewaltige Massiv der mehrgipfligen Meije (3983 m) erhebt. Alle bedeutenden Hochgipfel der Alpen waren schon bestiegen, als sie immer noch vergeblich berannt wurde. Ihre Besteigung 1877 gilt als die Großtat des frühen französischen Alpinismus (Boileau de Castelnau mit Vater und Sohn Gaspard). Nicht minder Eingang in die alpine Geschichte hat die erste Überschreitung des Berges durch die Österreicher Ludwig Purtscheller und Emil und Otto Zsigmondy 1885 gefunden, denn sie führten diese große Tour zu einer Zeit, als der Bergführer noch selbstverständlicher Begleiter war, als „Führerlose" aus; wenige Tage später fand Dr. Emil Zsigmondy, der Verfasser des großen alpinen Lehrbuchs „Die Gefahren der Alpen", beim Versuch, auch die Südwand der Meije zu durchsteigen, den Tod. Höchster Berg der Gruppe und südlichster Viertausender der Alpen ist die Barre des Ecrins (4101 m); sie fiel 1864 Edward Whymper in einer Pause seines mehrjährigen „Kampfes ums Matterhorn" zu.

Abseits des Hochgebirges ragt in der Dauphiné ein merkwürdiger Felsberg auf, der Mont Aiguille (2097 m); er galt für unersteiglich, weil Felswände ihn auf allen Seiten umgeben. Aber König Karl VIII. von Frankreich befahl, und sein Kammerherr Antoine de Ville stieg am 25. Juni 1492 mit etlichen Gefährten unter Einsatz von Seilen und Leitern durch die 300 m hohe Steilwand. An Ort und

8

Stelle schrieb Herr de Ville einen Bericht über seinen „fürchterlichsten und grauenerregendsten Weg" — einen Vorläufer der heutigen Tourenschilderungen.

Bevor der Alpenkamm aus der Süd-Nord-Richtung in die West-Ost-Richtung umschwenkt, wird er in den *Grajischen Alpen* schmäler. Über den Grenzkamm verbindet die Straße über den Kleinen St. Bernhard (2188 m) das Isèretal mit dem Aostatal. Inmitten des Steinbockreviers des Italienischen Nationalparks finden wir den höchsten Berg der Gruppe, einen der schönsten und leichtesten Viertausender, das „Große Paradies" (Gran Paradiso, 4061 m). Frankreich wartet in den Grajischen Alpen abermals mit Skiparadiesen von Weltrang auf; jeder deutsche Skiläufer, der auf sich hält, muß einmal in Val d'Isère und Courchevel Abfahrtskilometer gesammelt haben.

Jenseits des Aostatales bäumen sich die Alpen zu ihren höchsten Höhen auf: Rund um den „Monarchen" Mont Blanc (4807 m) ragen in den *Savoyer Alpen* über ein Dutzend Viertausender und eine verwirrende Fülle weiterer Gipfel — darunter viele Kletternadeln („Aiguilles") — auf. Zwischen den beiden Hauptorten Chamonix und Courmayeur kann man heute durch den Berg (Mont-Blanc-Tunnel, 11,6 km) oder mit Hilfe eines Seilbahnnetzes über seine Gletscherwüsten hinweg fahren. Der höchste Berg Europas wurde als erster ganz großer Hochgipfel erstiegen; der Dorfarzt von Chamonix Dr. Paccard und der bergbesessene Jacques Balmat holten sich am 8. August 1786 den Preis, den der Genfer Professor H. B. de Saussure für die Besteigung ausgesetzt hatte. Saussure selbst stand mit großem Gefolge — darunter Balmat — am 3. August 1787 auf der Schneekalotte; die alpine Geschichtsschreibung vergab hierfür (und nicht für die Erstbesteigung!) das Prädikat „Geburtstag des Alpinismus". Die Beschreibung der seitdem auf den Mont Blanc selbst und auf alle übrigen Gipfel der Gruppe gefundenen (meist schwierigen) Anstiege füllt ein dreibändiges Führerwerk; keine Wand, kein Grat blieb unbestiegen, und sogar durch die Nordwand der Grandes Jorasses gibt es heute verschiedene Routen. Ein „Unmöglich" kennt der Bergsteiger dank der technischen Hilfsmittel und der ausgefeilten Kletter- und Eistechnik nicht mehr.

Die *Walliser Alpen* zwischen dem Großen St. Bernhard (2473 m) und dem Simplon (2005 m) stehen den Savoyer Alpen an landschaftlicher Schönheit und an Bedeutung für Bergsteiger und Skiläufer nicht nach; an Fläche, Ausmaß der Vergletscherung und Zahl der Viertausender übertreffen sie diese bei weitem. Ihr höchstes Bergmassiv — eine ganze Krone von Gipfeln — ist der Monte Rosa (Dufourspitze 4634 m), doch wer Walliser Berge sagt, meint das Matterhorn (4477 m). Filme und Romane haben die dramatischen Ersteigungsgeschichten dieser zwischen Zermatt und Breuil (heute nach dem ital. „Cervino" benannten Berg in Cervinia umgetauft) aufragenden ebenmäßigen Pyramide populär gemacht: den Wettstreit zwischen dem Engländer Edward Whymper und dem italienischen Bergführer Jean Antoine Carrel, die Ersteigung am 14. Juli 1865 durch Whympers Mannschaft, während gleichzeitig Carrel auf dem von Breuil heraufführenden Grat bereits knapp unter dem Gipfel war — und schließlich die Katastrophe beim Abstieg, der vier der sieben Erstbesteiger zum Opfer fielen. Nochmals stand das Matterhorn im Mittelpunkt des Interesses, als die Münchner Brüder Franz und Toni Schmid 1931 seine Nordwand durchstiegen; sie waren aus Geldmangel mit dem Fahrrad in die Schweiz gekommen. Erstmals vergab das Olympische Komitee Goldmedaillen an Bergsteiger, doch Toni Schmid durfte ihre Überreichung 1932 nicht mehr erleben. Zermatt, Saas-Fee und Cervinia gehören zu den großen Skistationen der Alpen; die Bergbahnen und Lifte überschreiten hier die Dreitausend-Meter-Grenze mehrfach, und schon stehen die nächsten Ziele fest: Kleines Matterhorn (3883 m) von Zermatt, Feekopf (3888 m) von Saas-Fee: Chamonix mit seiner Bahn auf die Aiguille du Midi (3842 m) muß doppelt übertrumpft werden!

Im großen Zug der Südlichen Schweizer Alpen folgen auf die Walliser Alpen die Gruppen der *Lepontinischen Alpen* (Monte Leone, 3558 m) und der *Adula-Alpen* (Rheinwaldhorn, 3406 m), die am Splügen die Ostgrenze der Westalpen erreichen; ihnen parallel verläuft jenseits des Rhonetals die Kette der Nördlichen Schweizer Alpen mit den *Chablais-Alpen* (Dent du Midi, 3260 m) am Genfer

See, den *Freiburger* (Wildhorn, 3248 m), *Berner* und *Glarner Alpen* (Tödi, 3623 m). Furka- und Oberalppaß verknüpfen Rhein- und Rhonetal, während zwischen dem Vierwaldstätter See und der südlichen Berg- und Seenwelt des Tessins Bahn und Straße über den bzw. unter dem St. Gotthard (2112 m) die große Nord-Süd-Verbindung herstellen. Weiter westlich quert die Lötschberg-Simplon-Bahn die Alpen in zwei Tunnels auf der Strecke Kandersteg—Brig—Domodossola. Nur im Sommer frei ist der Grimselpaß (2165 m) zur Fahrt vom Berner Oberland ins oberste Rhonetal; der 1967 eröffnete Tunnel unter dem San Bernardino hat dem östlich parallel dazu verlaufenden Splügenpaß den großen Verkehr vom Hinterrheintal zu den oberitalienischen Seen abgenommen.

Nach ihrer Höhenlage, Vergletscherung und touristischen Bedeutung nehmen die *Berner Alpen* unter den Nördlichen Schweizer Alpen den ersten Rang ein. Hier finden wir noch einmal neun selbständige Viertausender mit dem Finsteraarhorn (4273 m) an der Spitze und den größten Gletscher der Alpen, den 115 qkm großen Aletschgletscher. Im Blickfeld der Hauptstadt Bern, hoch über den Wintersportplätzen Grindelwald, Wengen und Mürren, ragt das berühmteste Dreigestirn der Alpen auf: Eiger, Mönch und Jungfrau. Die Jungfraubahn fährt großenteils im Innern von Eiger und Mönch zum 3454 m hohen Jungfraujoch, von dem aus die Besteigung von Jungfrau (4158 m) und Mönch (4099 m) für geübte Bergsteiger nicht mehr allzu schwierig ist. Eine seltsame Faszination aber übt die als „Mordwand" berüchtigte Eiger-Nordwand auf die „Extremen" aus aller Welt aus: Von 1935 bis 1969 hat sie 35 Tote gefordert, etwa 200 Alpinisten haben sie seit der Erstbegehung durch Heckmair, Vörg, Harrer und Kasparek 1938 durchstiegen, und die Ersteigungen im Winter (1961), auf der „Winter-Direttissima" (1966) und schließlich der „Sommer-Direttissima" der Japaner (1969) sorgten immer wieder für Sensationen — von den Unfällen und großen Rettungsaktionen, vom ersten Alleingeher (1963) und der ersten Frau (1964) ganz abgesehen.

Mit einem Blick auf Engelberg mit seiner Bahn zum Titlis, die berühmten Aussichtsberge Pilatus und Rigi über dem Vierwaldstätter See, auf die Schweizer Urkantone — den Schauplatz von Friedrich Schillers „Wilhelm Tell" —, auf Säntis und Alpstein mit den Klettergipfeln der Kreuzberge westlich des Bodensees, auf die Churfirsten am Walensee, den Ideal-Skiberg Piz Sol über dem Rheintal und auf die große Wintersportstation Flims—Waldhaus verlassen wir endgültig die Westalpen.

Ostalpen

Wenn wir auch den Rhein überschritten haben, verbleiben wir zunächst noch in der Schweiz. Von der Graubündner Hauptstadt Chur führen die Straßen über Lenzerheide—Oberhalbstein—Julierpaß sowie die Rhätische Bahn durch den Albula-Tunnel ins Oberengadin. Der Name „*Plessur-Alpen*" ist kaum bekannt, doch die „Schneeschale" von Arosa in ihrem Herzen und das Parsenngebiet oberhalb Davos an ihrem Ostrand haben Weltruf. Pistenbetrieb spielt sich bei den *Oberhalbsteiner Alpen* (Piz Platta, 3398 m) und bei den zwischen Julier- und Flüela-Paß weitausgedehnten *Albula-Alpen* (Piz Kesch, 3420 m) nur am Rande ab, doch Bergsteiger und Skitouristen wissen diese noch meist einsame Bergwelt zwischen Davos und St. Moritz zu schätzen.

Südlich von St. Moritz und Pontresina, zwischen Malojapaß (1815 m) und Berninapaß (2323 m), liegt im Grenzbereich zwischen der Schweiz und Italien die *Berninagruppe*. Hier erheben sich die Ostalpen im Piz Bernina (4049 m) zu ihrem einzigen Viertausender. Der Schweizer Forstmann Johann Coaz erstieg ihn 1850 zum ersten Mal; den schönsten Weg zu diesem prachtvollen Berg — über die Firnschneide des Biancogrates und die abschreckende Berninascharte — beging 1878 der Berliner Dr. Paul Güßfeldt mit zwei einheimischen Führern. Vielbesucht von Bergsteigern und Skitouristen ist der dreigipfelige Piz Palü (3905 m), während die Pistenfahrer sich im Seilbahnbereich der Diavolezza und des Piz Corvatsch — zwei Aussichtspunkten von Weltrang — tummeln. Den schönsten Blick auf die durch ihre eisenfesten Granitkanten (Piz Badile u.a.) bei den Kletterern in höchster

10

Gunst stehenden Bergell-Berge bietet das Dörfchen Soglio, wo einst Segantini malte und wo heute Herr Jedermann ganze Filme verknipst.

Den Block der sechs Gebirgsgruppen im Westen der Ostalpen, östlich von dem die einst vom DÖAV eingeführte und allen Führerwerken zugrundeliegende Einteilung der Ostalpen in nicht weniger als 60 Gruppen einsetzt, beschließen die *Livigno-Alpen* (Cima di Piazzi, 3439 m) zwischen Samedan und Bormio und im Süden die weiträumigen *Bergamasker Alpen* (Pizzo di Scais, 3040 m) zwischen Sondrio und Bergamo.

Mag vieles in der Einteilung der Alpen noch umstritten sein, die große Dreiteilung der Ostalpen in Nördliche Kalkalpen, Zentralalpen und Südalpen ergibt sich aus den geologischen Gegebenheiten und ist allseits anerkannt. Wir wollen in unserm Blick auf die Alpen im folgenden jeweils diesen drei großen Zügen von West nach Ost folgen.

In den *Nördlichen Kalkalpen* liegt der gesamte deutsche Alpenanteil; er zieht sich als schmaler Streifen an ihrem Nordrande zwischen Bodensee und Königssee an der österreichischen Grenze entlang. Den westlichsten Block bildet die das Lechtal als langgezogenes Hufeisen umklammernde Bergwelt des *Bregenzerwald- und Lechquellengebirges*, der *Allgäuer* und *Lechtaler Alpen*. Eine Spezialität der Allgäuer Alpen sind steile Grasberge wie die Höfats, deren Edelweißreichtum den Sommer über von einem Bergwachtposten bewacht wird. Die wichtigsten Skigebiete finden sich im Norden um Hindelang, Oberstdorf und das Kleine Walsertal (das staatsrechtlich zu Österreich, wirtschaftlich jedoch zu Bayern gehört) und im Süden um den Arlbergpaß; hier — in St. Anton und St. Christoph — wurde der moderne alpine Skilaufstil entwickelt. Die Parseierspitze (3038 m) in den Lechtalern ist der einzige Dreitausender der Nördlichen Kalkalpen; höchster Berg der Allgäuer ist nicht die viel bekanntere Mädelegabel, sondern der Gr. Krottenkopf (2657 m).

Östlich des Lechdurchbruchs bei Füssen schließen sich die meist noch ruhigen *Ammergauer Berge* an, zu deren Füßen die Königsschlösser Neuschwanstein und Linderhof sowie das Passionsdorf Oberammergau Besucher aus aller Welt anziehen. Die langgedehnten *Bayerischen Voralpen* bieten im Münchner Nahausfluggebiet Tummelplätze vor allem des Massenskilaufs: Lenggries mit dem Brauneck, das Tegernseer Tal, den Spitzing und Bayrischzell mit Sudelfeld und Wendelstein. Sie sind den wesentlich höheren und bergsteigerisch ungleich wichtigeren Gruppen des *Wettersteins* und der *Mieminger*, des *Karwendels* und (östlich des größten Tiroler Sees, des Achensees) des *Rofans* vorgelagert. Zum deutschen Olympia-Ort Garmisch-Partenkirchen mit seiner Vielzahl von Bahnen und Liften — darunter auf Deutschlands höchsten Berg, die von drei Bergbahnen überzogene Zugspitze (2964 m) — treten als Ferienorte und Wintersportplätze Mittenwald, Seefeld und südlich des Karwendels die Tiroler Haupt- und Olympiastadt Innsbruck. Der Reichtum des Wettersteins an alpinhistorisch bedeutsamen Klettertouren läßt sich hier nicht einmal andeuten; im brüchigeren Karwendel (Birkkarspitze, 2756 m) genießt die Riesenmauer der Laliderer Wände bei den Alpinisten höchstes Ansehen.

Diese Feststellung gilt insgesamt auch für die jenseits des Inns bei Kufstein aufragende kleinste Gruppe der Ostalpen, das *Kaisergebirge*. In seiner Südhälfte, dem Wilden Kaiser, sind nur wenige Gipfel dem Bergwanderer zugänglich, während Berge wie das Totenkirchl, die Fleischbank und der Predigtstuhl mit ihren prallen Wänden und steilen Graten in die alpine Geschichte eingegangen sind; hier und in den Dolomiten wurde die Klettertechnik zu ihrem heutigen Stand entwickelt.

Die *Chiemgauer Alpen* im Norden mit Ski- und Ferienplätzen wie Reit im Winkl (Winklmoosalm) und Ruhpolding, wo der Sozialtourismus Furore gemacht hat, die einsamen Kalkklötze der *Leoganger* und *Loferer Steinberge* im Süden leiten zur östlichsten deutschen Gebirgsgruppe mit Hochgebirgscharakter über, zu den *Berchtesgadener Alpen*. Ihr höchster Berg, der Hochkönig (2938 m) steht allerdings auf österreichischem Boden, doch ihr Wahrzeichen ist der „König Watzmann" (2714 m), einer der charakteristischsten Berge Bayerns. Seine 1800 m hohe Ostwand — die höchste Wand der Ostalpen! — steilt über dem vom sommerlichen Fremdenverkehrsrummel überfluteten Kleinod Königssee auf; der Ramsauer Bergführer Johann Grill, genannt Kederbacher, führte schon 1881 den Wiener Otto Schück durch diese Riesenwand. Der Hochkalter mit dem Blaueis, dem einzigen deutschen und dem nördlichsten Gletscher der Alpen, sowie die weite Hochfläche des Steinernen Meers — ein Paradies der Tourenskiläufer — seien aus der den Markt Berchtesgaden umgebenden Bergwelt noch erwähnt; an ihrem Nordfuß liegen Bad Reichenhall und Salzburg.

Das *Tennengebirge* und die *Dachsteingruppe* bergen gewaltige Eishöhlen in ihrem Innern. Am Hohen Dachstein (2996 m) finden wir die letzte Vergletscherung, den letzten Aufschwung bis fast zur 3000-m-Grenze der Nördlichen Kalkalpen. Die Mauer der Dachstein-Südwand und die Felszacken des Gosaukamms ziehen die Kletterer von München bis Wien an. Die Verbindung der Seilbahnen von Norden (Obertraun—Krippenstein) und von Süden (Ramsau—Hunerkogel) wird nur eine Frage der Zeit sein; Fremdenverkehrsinteressen haben schon bei der Südwandbahn den weltweiten Protest der Naturschützer überspielt.

Weiter nach Osten werden die Berge immer niedriger, bis sie im Wienerwald in eine Hügelwelt auslaufen. Von den 10 Gruppen zwischen dem vielbesuchten Ferienland des Salzkammerguts und Wien haben noch größere bergsteigerische oder skiläuferische Bedeutung das riesige Plateau des *Toten Gebirges* (Hoher Priel, 2514 m), die *Ennstaler Alpen* (oder Gesäuse; Hochtor, 2373 m) als das Kletterparadies der Wiener über dem Ennsdurchbruch, die *Hochschwabgruppe* für die steirischen Kletterer und schließlich *Rax und Schneeberg* als Wiener Hausberge; diese beiden zuletzt genannten Gruppen stehen über dem Semmering, über den seit 1848 die Semmeringbahn Wien mit der Steiermark verbindet.

*

Das kleinste Alpenland, das Fürstentum Liechtenstein, bildet den Westrand des *Rätikons* und damit der *Zentralalpen*; über den Hauptkamm dieser Gruppe und ihren höchsten Berg, die Scesaplana (2969 m), verläuft die Grenze zwischen der Schweiz und Vorarlberg. Das „Skistadion Montafon" wird von den Skiläufern, die Südwände zwischen Drusenfluh und Sulzfluh werden von den Kletterern hochgeschätzt. Die unmittelbar anschließende *Silvretta* zeigt durch ihre starke Vergletscherung ein ganz anderes Landschaftsbild; im Frühjahr sind hier alle Hütten überfüllt. Ihr höchster Berg, der Piz Linard (3414 m), liegt ganz auf Schweizer Boden und überragt das Unterengadin; auf der Dreiländerspitze treffen sich Graubünden, Vorarlberg und Tirol. Zur Silvretta gehört zwar das Skigebiet Motta-Naluns über Schuls (Scuol), nicht aber das der Idalpe, zu der von Ischgl die „Silvrettabahn" führt; hier befinden wir uns bereits in der kleinen *Samnaun-Gruppe* (Muttler, 3298 m), in der das Zollausschlußgebiet des Samnauntales weithin bekannt ist. Diese Besonderheit geht auf die Zeit zurück, als das schweizerische Hochtal nur über österreichischen Boden erreicht werden konnte. Heute führt ein schmales Sträßchen von der Inntal-Straße herauf; sogar ein Auto mit einem großen Schiffsanhänger, dessen Fahrer sicher auch nur die Möglichkeit des billigen Einkaufens und Tankens ausnützen wollte, habe ich einmal dort den Verkehr behindern sehen. Jenseits des Paznauntales, aus dem die Silvretta-Hochalpenstraße ins Montafon führt, vervollständigt das *Ferwall* (Kuchenspitze, 3170 m) den Gebirgsblock zwischen Rhein, Arlberg und Inn.

Die größte Vergletscherung der Ostalpen findet sich in den *Ötztaler Alpen*, die den großen Raum zwischen Reschen und Timmelsjoch, zwischen Inn und Etsch einnehmen. Hier wie in den östlich (bis zum Brenner) anschließenden *Stubaier Alpen* läuft die österreichisch-italienische Grenze über den Hauptkamm. Vom Norden ziehen Kauner-, Pitz-, Ötz-, Sellrain- und Stubaital in das Innere des Gebirges; sie sorgen für eine starke Gliederung in Seitenkämme. Beide Gebirgsgruppen sind für Bergsteiger und Skiläufer von größtem Interesse; Zentren des Pistenskilaufs sind Sölden und Obergurgl im Ötztal, während Vent sowie drüben im Stubai Fulpmes und Neustift alte Bergsteigerdörfer darstellen. Aus der großen Gipfelflur beider Gruppen, die allein auf nordtiroler Seite einschließlich der Grenzgipfel 256 Dreitausender in den

Ötztalern und 151 in den Stubaiern umfaßt, seien Wildspitze (3774 m) und Weißkugel (3745 m) in den Ötztalern, Zuckerhütl (3507 m) und Schrankogel (3495 m) in den Stubaiern genannt. Schwierige Kletterberge weisen der Kaunergrat zwischen Pitz- und Kaunertal sowie die Kalkkögel — ein Kalkeinschiebsel im Urgestein der Zentralalpen über den Olympiapisten der Axamer Lizum und überm Stubaital — auf. Südliche Vorlagerungen dieses riesigen Gebirgssystems sind als selbständige Gebirgsgruppen im Südosten das ruhige Wandergebiet der *Sarntaler Alpen* zwischen Bozen und Sterzing, Meran und Brixen sowie im Südwesten die *Sesvennagruppe*. Piz Sesvenna und Piz Lischana dominieren hier im Dreiländereck zwischen Reschen- und Ofenpaß, in dem der größte Teil des Schweizer Nationalparks liegt.

Östlich des wichtigsten Ostalpenpasses, des von Eisenbahn und bald auch Autobahn überquerten Brenners (1370 m), folgen das wilde Hochgebirge der *Zillertaler Alpen* (Hochfeiler, 3523 m) und als ihre skifreundliche nördliche Vorlagerung die *Tuxer Alpen*. Bergbahnen und Lifte im Zillertal (Mayrhofen), im Tuxer- und Gerlostal sowie an den altberühmten Skibergen Patscherkofel und Glungezer locken immer mehr Skiläufer an. In dieser Beziehung werden die Zillertaler und Tuxer Alpen allerdings noch übertroffen von den *Kitzbühler Alpen*, auf deren meist sanfte Schieferberge aus fast allen Tälern die Lifte surren. Kitzbühel selbst und Saalbach/Hinterglemm sind Wintersportplätze von internationalem Rang; Zell am See mit der Schmittenhöhe, Kirchberg, Hopfgarten, Alpbach und die Wildschönau sowie viele kleinere Orte in der durch die Straße über den Paß Thurn in zwei Hälften geteilten Gruppe lassen auch Leute mit kleinerem Geldbeutel an den Freuden des Skilaufs teilnehmen.

Ohne auffallende Zäsur schließt sich an die Zillertaler Alpen das vielfach untergliederte System der *Hohen Tauern an*; an Länge wird dieses von den weiter im Osten folgenden *Niederen Tauern* übertroffen. Noch einmal umgibt ein weiter Gletschermantel die Hauptgipfel der Hohen Tauern; die Pasterze zwischen dem höchsten Berg Österreichs, dem Großglockner (3798 m), und dem bunten Treiben an der Franz-Josefs-Höhe, dem End-

punkt der von der Großglockner-Hochalpenstraße abzweigenden „Gletscherstraße", ist sogar der größte Gletscher der Ostalpen. Neben der 1935 eröffneten Glocknerstraße (Scheitelpunkt 2505 m), die Bruck im Pinzgau mit Heiligenblut verbindet, queren die neue Felbertauernstraße zwischen Mittersill und Osttirol in einem 5,2 km langen Tunnel sowie der schon 1908 gebohrte 8,5 km lange Eisenbahntunnel zwischen Mallnitz in Kärnten und dem Gasteiner Tal die Hohen Tauern; die Straßen über den Radstädter Tauern — auf dem sich der neue Ort Obertauern zum Wintersportplatz ersten Ranges entwickelt hat — und über den Rottenmanner Tauern führen über die Niederen Tauern. Ein geistlicher Würdenträger, der Fürstbischof von Gurk Altgraf Salm-Reifferscheid, gab gegen Ende des 18. Jahrhunderts den Auftrag zur Besteigung des Großglockners; Stützpunkte wurden errichtet, 1799 ein Kreuz auf dem Vorgipfel Kleinglockner errichtet und 1800 der Hauptgipfel erreicht. Schon 1876 stieg der Markgraf Alfred Pallavicini aus Wien mit drei Führern durch die nach ihm benannte Steilrinne zur Scharte zwischen Klein- und Großglockner; der Führer Josef Tribusser soll damals allein 2500 Stufen in das Eis der Rinne geschlagen haben. Der „weltalten Majestät" des Großvenedigers (3674 m) rückte 1828 Erzherzog Johann vergeblich zu Leibe; erst 1841 erstieg eine ganze Expedition unter Führung des Pflegers von Mittersill J. v. Kürsinger das bis in die oberbayerische Hochebene sichtbare Gletscherdach. Eine neue Ära der Eistechnik begann 1924, als der Münchner Stadtbaurat Dr. Willo Welzenbach bei der Erstbegehung der Nordwestwand des Gr. Wiesbachhorns erstmals Eishaken verwendete.

Im Kapruner Tal am Fuß dieser Wand finden wir heute gewaltige Stauwerke (Mooserboden- und Limbergsperre) und die Seilbahn auf über 3000 m Höhe, die am Gr. Kitzsteinhorn Sommerskibetrieb ermöglicht. Zu den Hohen Tauern zählen außer *Glockner-* und *Venediger-Gruppe* die zwischen beiden gelegene *Granatspitzgruppe* (Gr. Muntanitz, 3231 m), weiter im Osten *Goldberg-* (Hocharn, 3251 m) und *Ankogel-Gruppe* (Hochalmspitze, 3355 m) sowie als südliche Vorlagerungen die *Rieserfernergruppe* mit dem wuchtigen Hochgall (3440 m), die *Villgratener*

Berge im Grenzkamm zwischen Ost- und Südtirol, die *Schober-* und die *Kreuzeck-Gruppe.* Die Niederen Tauern kulminieren im Hochgolling, 2863 m. In den *Norischen* und *Cetischen Alpen* laufen die Zentralalpen nach Osten aus.

*

Zum letzten Mal — diesmal durch die *Südlichen Ostalpen* — wollen wir unsern Gang von West nach Ost antreten. Östlich Bernina-, Livigno- und Bergamasker Alpen treffen wir auf zwei große Gletschergebiete und auf gewaltige Berge: auf die *Ortler-Gruppe* zwischen Vinschgau und Sulzbergtal sowie südlich davon auf die nach ihren beiden Hauptgipfeln *Adamello* (3554 m) und *Presanella* (3564 m) benannte Gebirgsgruppe. „König Ortler" (3902 m) und Königsspitze (3859 m) über den alten Südtiroler Bergsteigerdörfern (und heute natürlich Wintersportplätzen) Sulden und Trafoi gehören zu den höchsten und schönsten Gipfeln der Ostalpen; der Cevedale (3769 m) zählt zu den höchsten Skibergen der ganzen Alpen. Wie so mancher andere Hochgipfel wurde auch der Ortler auf Befehl eines hohen Herrn bestiegen; Erzherzog Johann gab den Auftrag, und der „Passeirer Josele" — der Gemsjäger Josef Pichler — fand am 27. September 1804 den Weg. Auf den Gletschern der Ortler- und der Adamello-Gruppe ebenso wie im unwegsamen Felsland der Dolomiten und der Karnischen Alpen spielte sich 1915—1918 ein erbitterter Hochgebirgskrieg ab, auf dessen Spuren der Bergsteiger heute noch in diesen Gebieten trifft. Strategische Gründe waren auch maßgebend beim Bau der Stilfserjochstraße; dieser höchste Straßenübergang der Ostalpen (2757 m) ist zwar im Winter geschlossen, doch ab Frühsommer spielt sich hier in einem Zirkus von Liften ein reger Sommerskibetrieb ab. Die in Nord-Süd-Richtung langgezogenen *Nonsberger Alpen* haben durch die in ihrem SW-Eck gelegenen Kletterberge der Brenta erhebliche touristische Bedeutung; Madonna di Campiglio ist ihr Zentrum, die Cima Tosa (3176 m) ihr höchster und der Campanile Basso („Guglia di Brenta") ihr berühmtester Berg. Die Bergsteiger rechnen die aus Dolomitgestein aufgebaute Brenta vielfach zu den Dolomiten; beide Gruppen sind jedoch durch

das weite Etschtal und durch die verhältnismäßig wenig besuchte Bergwelt der *Fleimstaler Alpen* getrennt. Die Dolomiten selbst füllen den großen Raum zwischen dem Pustertal im Norden und dem Eggental und Rollepaß im Süden; im Westen begrenzt sie der Eisack, während sie im Osten in die *Belluneser Alpen* übergehen. Südlich von Trient, von der Brenta und den Fleimstalern, nimmt die Bergwelt der *Brescianer* und *Gardasee-Gruppe* sowie (östlich der Etsch) der *Vicentiner Alpen* in Richtung Alpenrand an Höhe und Bedeutung ab.

Die vielfach untergliederten *Dolomiten* sind in wenigen Zeilen nicht zu erfassen. Ihr höchster Berg ist auch ihr vielseitigster: von Norden ist die Marmolata (3344 m) ein mit Bahnen und Liften erschlossener großartiger Skiberg, während ihre breite Südwand den extremen Kletterern vorbehalten bleibt. „Il regno del sesto grado" („Königreich des VI. Grades") nennen die Italiener die Civetta-Gruppe, doch noch mehr Aufsehen erregten die Begehungen der verschiedenen Kletterrouten durch die Nordwände der Drei Zinnen; die Anstiege der Münchner Solleder und Lettenbauer 1925 durch die Civetta-NW-Wand und der Italiener Comici und Brüder Dimai 1931 durch die Nordwand der Gr. Zinne leiteten hier ein neues Zeitalter des sportlichen Kletterns ein. Der Rosengarten mit den spitzen Vajolettürmen (deren kühnsten, den Winklerturm, der 17jährige Münchner Gymnasiast Georg Winkler 1887 als Alleingeher erstmals erklomm) schaut in die Straßen von Bozen; Zentrum der östlichen Dolomiten ist die Olympiastadt Cortina d'Ampezzo unter den Tofanen. Langkofel und Sella über dem Grödner Tal, dem Schauplatz der Skiweltmeisterschaften 1970, die Sextener Berge im Norden und nicht zuletzt im Süden die „wildschöne" Pala über San Martino di Castrozza — sie können die Zauberwelt der Dolomiten nur andeuten, aber keineswegs erschöpfen. Die hervorragenden Straßen, welche die Dolomiten über ihre großen Pässe (Grödner, Sella-, Pordoijoch, Falzaregopaß usw.) hinweg durchziehen, haben aus diesem einst unwegsamen Gebirge heute ein Reise- und Ferienland gemacht, wie es in den Alpen kaum irgendwo ähnlich anzutreffen ist; auch der Ski hat in diesem Felsgebirge eine Heimat gefunden.

Nicht viel kleiner als die Dolomiten, jedoch weniger erschlossen und nur an einigen Punkten – etwa dem „unlogischsten Berg der Alpen", dem Campanile di Val Montanaia – von Bergsteigern vielbesucht, ziehen sich die *Karnischen Alpen* jenseits der Piave nach Osten. In ihrem Hauptkamm, der die österreichisch-italienische Grenze trägt, liegen die höchsten Berge (Hohe Warte, 2787 m) und die meisten Hütten. Die Straßen über die einstige deutsche Sprachinsel Sappada und (südlicher) über den Mauriapaß queren den Südteil der Gruppe in Ost-West-Richtung.

Parallel zum Grenzkamm verläuft zwischen Gail und Drau der lange Zug der *Gailtaler Alpen*; er reicht von den schönen Kletterbergen der „Lienzer Dolomiten" über der Osttiroler Hauptstadt Lienz bis zum altberühmten Aussichtsberg Dobratsch über Villach.

Wir sind am Ost-Ende auch der Südalpen angelangt, im Grenzgebiet zwischen Österreich, Italien und Jugoslawien. Die letzten drei Gruppen gilt es hier zu erwähnen: die Kärnten und Slowenien trennenden *Karawanken* (Hochstuhl, 2239 m), die *Steiner Alpen* (Grintovec 2559 m), die mit Ausnahme eines kleinen Dreiecks, das in die Gruppe hineinstößt und den südlichsten Punkt Österreichs aufweist, ganz in Jugoslawien gelegen sind, und schließlich die *Julischen Alpen*. Sie stellen das touristisch bedeutendste Gebirge Jugoslawiens dar; etwa ein Drittel der Gebirgsgruppe gehört allerdings zu Italien. Der von Wischberg (2666 m) und Montasch (2752 m) überragte italienische Anteil ist vergleichsweise einsam geblieben, während die Slowenen ihrem höchsten Gebirge alle Liebe und Begeisterung zugewandt haben. Sie haben diese schöne Bergwelt bestens – und manchmal fast zu viel! – erschlossen und mitten durch schwierige Wände mit großem technischen Aufwand kühne Klettersteige gelegt; die zahlreichen Hütten des 1893 gegründeten Slowenischen Alpenvereins (Planinska zveza Slovenije) bieten allen Bergsteigern Gastfreundschaft. Den großen Erschließer der Julischen Alpen, den in Triest lebenden Österreicher Dr. Julius Kugy (1858–1944), verehren die Alpinisten aus den drei hier sich berührenden Nationen gleichermaßen; sein Denkmal steht in der Trenta, im Herzen der slowenischen Julier, unweit ihres höchsten Berges, des Triglav (2863 m). Die Kletterer, die seine 1500 m hohe Nordwand durchsteigen, treffen sich auf dem aussichtsreichen Gipfel mit unzähligen Alpinisten, die auf gesicherten Steigen von vier hochgelegenen Unterkunftshütten heraufgekommen sind. Die Täler der Wocheiner Save und des Isonzo (Soča) führen in das Gebirge, die interessanten Straßen über Vršič- und Predilpaß überqueren es. Zu den Glanzpunkten der Julier zählen der Wocheiner und der Veldeser (Bleder) See sowie die Perlenkette der sieben Triglavseen. Die Hochfläche der Komna bietet ein schönes Skigebiet; auf der Skiflugschanze von Planica wurde 1936 erstmals die 100-m-Grenze übersprungen.

*

Rund 1200 km Weges durch die Alpen von Nizza an der Côte d'Azur bis Laibach am Südfuß der Steiner Alpen liegen hinter uns. Mögen die Eindrücke noch so sehr gewechselt haben, als Ergebnis bleibt:

„Kein schöner Land ..."

*

Begleitworte wie dieses können und sollen den Betrachter der Bilder begleiten, sollen ihm sagen, was optisch nicht ausgedrückt zu werden vermag; sie können deshalb nicht zu einer erschöpfenden Darstellung einer Landschaft werden; sie ergänzen also nur das Bild. So kommt es, daß vieles ungesagt bleiben muß. Wenn der Raum eine breitere Schilderung versagt, dann möge der Leser bedenken, daß des Lesens und des Schauens wegen dieser Bildband geschaffen wurde.

THE ALPS

"The Alps, the Alps, whose memory
My heart keeps ever green"
Nikolaus Lenau, 1802—1850

"The playground of Europe"
Title of a book on mountains
by Leslie Stephen, 1871

The spiritual home of the poet or the sports ground of the serious mountaineer? Between these two poles we can find many tenable points of view respecting the Alps. Since the earliest days of science, they have given geographers, geologists, minerologists, glaciologists and many other scientists occasion to examine and to classify, to propound theories (as well as to counter these), and to write books about them.

The economic importance of the Alps formerly lay in their reserves of iron, salt or timber; today they are the holiday-playgrounds of Europe. Tourism has become a decisive economic factor for the alpine countries, its importance having been almost doubled by the spreading of skiing. In earlier days the Alps were the greatest obstacle to Continental communications. Since the days of the Romans, technicians have learned to overcome this by roads over passes, since mid 19th century, by railways. The tunnels have become longer and longer and the latest idea is to set up a network of mountain cable-railways over entire massifs.

Shepherds and hunters were doubtlessly the first men to penetrate into the higher regions of the Alps but the local population did not remain sole masters for long. They were outdone by intellectuals from the cities, who came as explorers — or pretended to be such, even when they were merely curious; a new attitude towards Nature gave a legitimate aspect to their curiosity and was a stimulus to alpinism as a mass movement.

This mass movement led to alpine societies not only in alpine lands but also beyond them. That the first of these in non-alpine lands was the Alpine Club established in London in 1857 was no coincidence, for the systematic opening up of the Alps, especially the Western Alps, was the work of English alpinists in the first place, even though they employed local guides. Unhasting, the mountaineers of the alpine lands followed them: in 1862, the Austrian Alpine Club (Ö.A.V.), in 1863, the Swiss Alpine Club (S.A.C.) and the Alpine Club of Italy (C.A.I.) too, in 1869, the German Alpine Club (D.A.V.) and in 1874, the French one, the "C.A.F.". The "D.A.V." and the "Ö.A.V." were united in the "D.Ö.A.V.", the German and Austrian Club from 1874 till 1945. Today, mountaineering clubs are to be found in almost every country in the world — be they never so flat: they call themselves "Alpine Clubs" however great the distance from the ancient Alps (as in New Zealand, Japan and the U.S.A.). As like-minded clubs tend to coalesce into supra-national associations, the mountaineering clubs of Europe and across the seas, of East and West (politically regarded) joined one another under the aegis of the "Union Internationale des Associations d'Alpinisme".

This mass movement again, stimulated art in many fields; it produced a voluminous alpine literature and many paintings of the Alps. No greater library of books on the Alps existed than the "Alpenvereinsbücherei" in Munich until, in 1943, it was largely destroyed; there were about 60,000 titles listed in its catalogue. It now has 24,000 titles again as well as 2,000 maps and a collection of periodicals dealing with the subject.

*

"The high mountain ranges of the Alps give Central Europe its singular and grand stature. Their influence extends on all sides far across the Continent... The Alps cool down Central Europe, considerably, it is true, but they compensate for this handsomely by the noble splendour of their contours, by the plentiful rainfall which waters the contiguous countries and by the singular impression of freshness and beauty that is theirs alone and which they diffuse around them. The Alps are the crown of Europe and their eternal snows the diamonds." With these poetic words the Prussian geographer, Captain H. Beitzke began his 902-page work, "The Alps"

(Colberg, 1843). Prosaically, the dictionary says "Alps, the highest mountain range in Europe, stretching from 43.5° to 48°N. and 3° to 16.5°E. From the Gulf of Genoa to Vienna and to the Julian Alps and the Gateway to the denuded Alps of Slovenia, they form a convex arc towards the west and eastwards a curve that flattens out. The breakaway of the Appennines is found at the Altare Pass (1506 ft) ... The Alps within this framework are about 808 miles long and between 93 and 155 miles wide and cover an area representing some 88,00 square miles on the map." (Brockhaus Encyclopedia, 1967 et seq.).

It was a matter of centuries before this information about the Alps was ascertained. The geographers of antiquity did not know how far the alpine curve really extended and as late as 1574, Josias Simler, a Swiss, wrote in "De alpibus commentarius", the first comprehensive book on the subject at all: "We adopt the opinion of the old writers who said: 'The Alps proper are those mountains that form the frontier of Italy'." Incidentally, Chapter XIV of this work, on 'Difficulties and Dangers of the Routes into the Alps and how to overcome them', represents the first text-book on mountaineering.

However much we may know about the Alps, nowadays, about their grouping there is still no unanimity. Against the earlier division which proposed three groups, the French-Italian Alps, the Swiss or Central Alps and the Eastern Alps, the more modern bisection, viz., into Eastern and Western Alps, has prevailed in general. That the boundary between these two crosses the Splügen Pass (Rhein, Hinterrhein, Splügen, Liro, Mera to Como) is really no longer much disputed among scientists, but for many an alpine writer it goes against the grain, for they "feel that, in view of their clearly recognisable West-Alpine scenic character, Bernina and Bergell are essentially part of the Western Alps" (K. Lukan, "Das Grosse Alpenbuch", 1969). The intuitive geographers frequently met with do not take into account, however, that with such an arbitrary eastward transposition of the boundary — to about the vicinity of the Swiss frontier — no natural division is to be found and that — even leaving out Bernina and Bergell—they will add to the Western Alps five mountain groups without West-Alpine character, viz., Plessur, Oberhalbstein, Albula, Livigno and Bergamo Alps.

If we take an imaginary flight over the Alps from the Mediterranean Sea to the Danube and make a survey of the most important mountain groups, the most interesting peaks, the places of note, the great routes and the outstanding events of alpine history, this systematic division of the Alps will only be a kind of rough guide. To outline an appreciation of all the individual alpine groups would go too far beyond the scope of this volume of pictures of the Alps. We beg the reader's indulgence also if, in the sphere of geology and such sciences, we forgo all claims to expertise beyond that commonly acknowledged as belonging to the general knowledge expected of an author.

The Western Alps

Above the palm-shaded promenades, the casinos and the meat-markets of the Riviera stand the peaks of the Ligurian and the Maritime Alps, which already rise, however, to a height of 10,817 ft in the latter, the highest peak being 'Punta' Argentera. Here, too, are the southernmost French winter-sports centres, Auron and Valberg; the short distance to Nice (56 mls) makes it possible to chase down their snowy slopes and then to water-ski on the waters of the Côte d'Azur in one day in spring.

The Lower Alps of Provence link up, limestone mountains without any high-alpine character. Here we find the Gorges du Verdon, the most stupendous ravine in Europe and a really superb view is obtained from Mont Ventoux (6173 ft). On this mountain began the history of mountaineering in the Alps. The poet, Francesco Petrarca, made the ascent with his brother Gerhard on April 26th, 1336. He wrote to Cardinal Colonna: "Yesterday, I climbed the highest mountain in our vicinity, which, not undeservedly, is called 'the windy one', my sole reason

being to acquaint myself with this peak of considerable altitude." He admitted, without reserve, that, in the last analysis, that passion had driven him which is the origin of all feats in alpine history. "This mountain, visible far and wide, rose before my eyes almost continuously until my longing gradually became fierce."

As an enormous block in which (proceeding from the south) the height of 4000 metres (13,124 ft) is exceeded for the first time, the Cottian and the Dauphiné Alps follow the Maritime and the Provence Alps. Turin in the east and Grenoble in the west are the gateways to these two important groups of mountains. The cross-connection between Italy and France is used by the railway line that is called after Mont Cenis, but actually it passes under the Col de Fréjus through a 7.5-mile tunnel. Motor traffic runs over the Col de Mont Cenis (between Susa and Lanslebourg it rises to 6833 ft) or over the Col de Montgenèvre, between Susa and Briançon. Those motorists specialising in passes will find an entire Motorists' Guide full of interesting passes in the French Alps, if they traverse these in longitudinal directions. The magnificent "Route des Alpes" alone, between Thonon on Lake Geneva and Nice, crosses over ten passes of which six rise higher than 6562 ft (the highest, Col d'Iseran at 9088 ft). Further west, the Route Napoléon connects Grenoble with Cannes.

In the Cottian Alps, named after the legendary King Cottius, there is one mountain and one place that are widely known: Monte Viso and Sestrière. On the lower slopes of this 12,602-ft Monte Viso, "the most isolated peak and the one that most mightily dominates its surroundings anywhere in the Alps", the River Po rises. Though the first ascent was by an Englishman with French guides in 1861, it is, none the less, felt to be Italian, more especially because on its summit, in 1863, that enthusiastic climber, the Minister Quintino Sella and his friends decided to found an Italian alpine club. From 1931 on, the first winter-sports centre to be blue-printed, Sestrière, was planned at the instigation of the Head of the FIAT Works, Senator Agnelli. Its towering hotels brought it fame.

Towards the west and still in sight from Sestrière, rise the Dauphiné Alps. Here, too, there are fully mechanised ski-paradises such as Alpe d'Huez, Les Deux Alpes and Chamrousse, but the name of Dauphiné sounds sweetest to the ears of mountaineers; their mecca is the little village of La Grave below the Col du Lauteret if it isn't the few houses in the remote La Bérade in Vénéon Valley between which places rises the huge massif of the Meije with several peaks (12,461 ft) (Massif du Pelvoux). All the other high alpine peaks of note had already been conquered when this massif was still being assaulted in vain. Its ascent in 1877 ranked as the greatest feat in French alpinism (Boileau de Castelnau with the Gaspards, senior and junior). The first crossing of the mountain by the Austrians, Ludwig Purtscheller with Emil and Otto Zsigmondy, in 1885, was found no less worthy of a place in the annals of alpine history, for they achieved this without a guide at a time when a guide was still considered essential. It was only a few days later that Dr. Emil Zsigmondy, the author of the great alpine text-book "The Dangers of the Alps", was killed attempting to climb the Meije up the South Wall route. The highest peak and the southernmost of Alpine peaks of 4000 ms is the Barre des Ecrins (13,455 ft); it was conquered by Edward Whymper in an interval between his struggles to conquer the Matterhorn, which took him several years.

Standing apart from the High Alps in the Dauphiné, there is a remarkable rocky pinnacle, Mont Aiguille (6880 ft); it long ranked as impregnable since all its faces were precipitous. But King Charles VIII of France issued a command and on June 25th, 1492, Antoine de Ville, his chamberlain, together with some companions climbed the sheer, 984-ft-rock face, with the aid of ropes and ladders. On the spot, de Ville wrote a report on "the most dreadful and horrifying path" – a foretaste of present-day tourists' descriptions.

Before the crest of the Alps changes direction from a longitudinal to a more latitudinal one, it becomes narrower in the Graian Alps. The Little St. Bernhard Pass (7178 ft) over the frontier on the crest joins the Isère Valley to the Aosta Valley. In the midst of the Italian

National Park, in the haunts of the ibex, there is one of the finest and easiest of the 'four-thousanders' (above 13,000 ft), the Gran Paradiso (13,323 ft). In the Graian Alps, France again offers elysian skiing grounds of international standard; any West-European who has his pride must have 'collected' downhill runs at least in Val d'Isère and Courcheval.

Beyond the Aosta Valley, the Alps are piled up to their greatest altitudes: round about the 'Monarch', Mont Blanc (15,781 ft), more than a dozen peaks in the Savoy Alps tower up to over 13,000 feet and an embarrassing choice of more summits – many among them are crags (Aiguilles) for rock-climbers. Between the two chief sports centres, Chamonix and Courmayeur, one can travel nowadays either through the mountain (Mont Blanc Tunnel, 7.25 mls long) or swing over its icy wastes by means of the network of cable-railways. The highest mountain in Europe was climbed as his first really high peak by the village doctor of Chamonix, Dr. Paccard and the mountain-obsessed Jacques Balmat, on August 8th, 1786, to obtain the prize offered by a Geneva professor, H. B. de Saussure, for the first conquest of Mont Blanc. On August 3rd, 1787, Saussure himself stood with a large following, including Balmat, on the snowy crown (Schneekalotte); this, and not the first ascent, was awarded the honour of counting as the 'birthday of alpinism' in the annals of alpine history. The description of various climbs up Mont Blanc itself and up all the other peaks in the group which have been found since then (mostly difficult ones) fills a guide-book of three volumes. There is no ridge and no wall that has been left unconquered and even over the North Wall of the Grandes Jorasses there are now several routes to choose from. Thanks to technical aids and perfected techniques of climbing rock and ice, the mountaineer no longer admits that there is such a thing as an 'impossible' climb.

The Pennine Alps between the Great St. Bernhard Pass (8113 ft) and the Simplon (6591 ft) are not inferior to the Savoy Alps in respect of scenic beauty nor of importance to the mountaineer and the skier, while they far exceed them in area, extent of glaciation and the number of peaks over 13,000 feet. Their highest massif—an entire crown of peaks—is Monte Rosa (Dufour Peak, 15,217 ft), but whoever speaks of the Pennine Alps thinks of the Matterhorn (14,705 ft). Films and novels have familiarized the public with the dramatic first ascent of this towering symmetrical pyramid between Zermatt and Breuil, now renamed Cervin after the Italian "Cervino". This drama was the competition between the Englishman, Edward Whymper and the Italian mountain guide, Jean Antoine Carrel, the ascent on July 14th, 1865 by Whymper's team, while at the same time, Carrel was just under the peak having climbed the arête from Breuil—and the disaster of the descent in which four of the seven victors became victims. Yet again the Matterhorn was the cynosure of interest when the two Munich brothers, Franz and Toni Schmid traversed its North Wall. Short of funds, they had cycled to Switzerland. Now, for the first time, the Olympic Committee awarded gold medals to mountaineers, but Toni Schmid was not to live for the presentation in 1932. Zermatt, Saas-Fee and Cervinia are among the great skiing centres in the Alps; here, the mountain railways and lifts go beyond 3000 metres altitude in many places and now the next ones are already planned: the Lower Matterhorn (12,739 ft) from Zermatt, and Feekopf (12,756 ft) from Saas-Fee. Chamonix with its railway to the Aiguille du Midi (12,605 ft) must be doubly over-trumped!

In the great sweep of the Swiss Alps, in the south, the Pennine Alps are followed by the group of Lepontine Alps (Monte Leone, 11,673 ft) and the Adula Alps (Rheinwaldhorn, 11,175 ft) which extend to the Splügen Pass, the boundary of the Western Alps. Parallel to these, however, on the other side of the Rhône Valley, there is the chain of the northern Swiss Alps, the Chablais Alps (Dent du Midi, 10,696 ft) above Lake Geneva, the Freiburg Alps (Wildhorn, 10,574 ft), Bernese and Glarner Alps (Tödi, 11,448 ft). The Furka and Oberalp Passes connect the Rhine and Rhône Valleys, while between Lake Lucerne and the southern world of lake and mountain in the Ticino, road and railway run over or under the St. Gotthard (6929 ft); these represent the great north to south connections. Further west the Lötschberg-Simplon railway crosses the Alps through two tunnels on the Kandersteg, Brig and Domodossola line. Only in summer is the Grimsel Pass (7103 ft) open to allow of crossing from the Bernese Oberland into the Upper Rhône Valley; the tunnel under the San Bernardino, opened in 1967, has relieved its eastern parallel, Splügen Pass, of the great volume of traffic from the Hinter Rhein Valley to the Upper Italian Lakes.

In accordance with their altitudes, the extent of their glaciation and their importance for tourism, the Bernese Alps take first place among the Alps of north Switzerland. Here we find a further nine separate mountains over 13,000 feet high, the Finsteraarhorn in the van (14,022 ft) and the largest glaciers in the Alps; 46 sq.mls is the area of the greatest, the Aletsch Glacier. Within view of the capital, Bern, and rising high above the winter-sports centres of Grindelwald, Wengen and Mürren, shines the most famous alpine constellation: the three stars of the Eiger, Mönch and Jungfrau. The Jungfrau Railway runs mostly inside the Eiger and Mönch up to the Jungfraujoch (11,342 ft), from which point the ascents of the Jungfrau itself (13,645 ft) and of Mönch (13,386 ft) are no longer too difficult for experienced climbers. The notorious North Wall of the Eiger exercises a singular fascination on climbing devotees from all over the world; between 1935 and 1969 it claimed 35 victims, but some 200 alpinists have traversed it since the first ascent by Heckmair, Vörg, Harrer and Kasparek in 1938, while the ascents in winter (1961), via the Winter "Direttissima"—the fall line—in 1966—and finally via the Summer "Direttissima" by Japanese in 1969 inevitably provided sensations, quite apart from the accidents and large-scale rescue operations, the first solo climber (1963) and the first woman to reach the summit (1964).

With a glance at Engelberg with its railway to the Titlis; Pilatus, famous for its splendid views, as well as Rigi, above Lake Lucerne, a glance, too, at the first Swiss cantons, the scene of Friedrich Schiller's "William Tell", and at Säntis and Alpstein with the crags of the Kreuzbergs, west of Lake Constance, towards the Churfirsten on Lake Walen, not omitting the ideal skiing mountain, Piz Sol above the Rhine Valley nor the winter-sports centre, Flims-Waldhaus, we must finally leave the Western Alps.

The Eastern Alps

Even though we have crossed the Rhine, we still remain in Switzerland. From Chur, the capital of Grisons, the roads lead via Lenzerheide, Oberhalbstein and the Julier Pass or, as does the Rhaetian Railway, through the Albula Tunnel into the Upper Engadine. The name "Plessur" Alps is scarcely known, but the "Snow Bowl" of Arosa, in their midst, and the Parsenn area above Davos and on their eastern edge are internationally renowned. Downhill skiing slopes are merely a side-line in the case of the Oberhalbstein Alps (Piz Platta, 11,148 ft) or the extensive Albula Alps between the Julier and the Flüela Passes (Piz Kesch, here is 11,220 ft high) but the mountaineers and touring skiers hold in high esteem this area between Davos and St. Moritz; it is mostly still a quiet, unfrequented mountain region.

South of St. Moritz and Pontresina, between the Maloja Pass (5955 ft) and the Bernina Pass (7645 ft), on the Swiss-Italian frontier lies the Bernina Group. Here the Eastern Alps rise to their only peak above 13,000 feet, viz., Piz Bernina (13,304 ft). A Swiss forester, Johann Coaz, first made the ascent in 1850 but the finest route up this magnificent mountain, i.e., via the névé knife-edge of the Bianco Ridge and the forbidding Bernina Fissure, was first climbed by the Berliner, Dr. Paul Güssfeldt with local guides, in 1878. Piz Palü (12,812 ft) with its three peaks is much frequented by mountaineers and touring skiers, while those preferring the beaten tracks of the downhill slopes disport themselves within reach of the cable railways on Diavolezza and Piz Corvatsch—peaks with supremely fine views. The Bergell Mountains, high favourites with the climbers on account of their firm, iron-hard granite edges (Piz Badile among others) are

seen to best advantage from the little village of Soglio, where Segantini once painted and where today, entire films are used up by every holiday-maker.

The block of the six mountain groups in the west of the Eastern Alps is still east of the dividing line once introduced by the Austro-German Alpine Club and still in all the guide-books; this left no fewer than 60 groups in the east section. This last block ends with the Livigno Alps (Cina di Piazzi, 11,283 ft) between the Samedan and Bormio and, in the south, the long range of the Bergamo Alps (Pizzo di Scais, 9974 ft) between Sondrio and Bergamo.

With regard to the line dividing the Alps, there may still be much that is debatable, but the great tripartition of the Eastern Alps into the Northern, Limestone Alps, the Central and the Southern Alps results from geological factors and is accepted on all sides. In our survey of the Alps below, we shall follow these three great ranges from west to east.

In the Northern, Limestone Alps all of the German section is contained; it stretches along their north edge, a narrow strip between Lakes Constance and Königssee and there along the Austrian frontier. The westernmost block comprises the long horseshoe of ranges enveloping the Lech Valley, the Alps of the Bregenz Forest and the Lech Sources, and the Allgau and the Lech Valley Alps. A peculiarity of the Allgau Alps is their steep but grassy mountains such as the Höfats where the treasured edelweiß are watched over all summer by the Mountain Rescue Service. The most important skiing areas are north of Hindelang, Oberstdorf and Klein Walsertal (which belongs politically to Austria but economically to Germany) as well as in the south, round the Arlberg Pass where, in St. Anton and St. Christoph, the modern style of skiing was developed. The Parseier Spitze (9968 ft) in the Lech Valley Alps is the only one approaching 10,000 feet in the North Limestone Alps. The highest mountain in the Allgau Alps is not the much better-known one, Mädelegabel, but Great Krottenkopf (8717 ft).

East of where the Lech breaks through near Füssen, come the mostly still peaceful Oberammergau Mountains at whose feet are the royal castles of Neuschwanstein and Linderhof, which, like the Passion-Play village of Oberammergau itself, attracts visitors from all over the world. The long drawn-out foothills of the Bavarian Alps offer a playground for Munich excursionists, above all for the massed skiers: Lenggries with Brauneck, the Tegernsee Valley, Spitzing and Bayrischzell with Sudelfeld and Wendelstein. These extend in front of the considerably higher and, for the mountaineer, far more important groups of the Wetterstein, the Mieming and the Karwendel Ranges and, east of the largest lake in Tyrol, Achensee, the Rofan Group. Garmisch-Partenkirchen, once the scene of the Olympic Winter Games, has an abundance of mountain railways and skilifts, some going up Germany's highest mountain, the Zug Spitze (9738 ft), which alone has three mountain railways. In addition to Garmisch-Partenkirchen, there are the holiday and winter-sports centres of Mittenwald, Seefeld and, south of the Karwendels, Innsbruck, the capital of Tyrol and one-time arena for the Olympic Sports. The Wetterstein Range's wealth in respect of historically important alpine climbing tours can be no more than mentioned here. In the more crumbly rocks of the Karwendel (Birkkar Peak, 9042 ft), the gigantic rock-faces of the Lalider Walls have gained the highest respect of alpinists.

This claim is generally valid, too, for the smallest group of the Eastern Alps, the Kaiser Mountains, which rise beyond the River Inn near Kufstein. In its southern half, the Wild Kaiser, there are few peaks accessible to the mountain walker, while mountains such as the 'Totenkirchl', the 'Fleischbank', and the 'Predigtstuhl' (Pulpit) with their imposing precipitous faces and steeply sloping ridges have been entered in the annals of alpine history. Here, and in the Dolomites, the techniques of scaling have been developed up to their present standard.

The Chiemgau Alps in the north, with their skiing and holiday centres such as Reit im Winkl (Winkelmoosalm) and Ruhpolding where mass tourism has developed sensationally, and, in the south, the isolated limestone masses of the Leogang and Lofer Steingebirge (Rocky Mts.) bridge the gap to the eastern German mountain groups of high-alpine character, viz., the Berchtesgaden Alps. Their highest peak, Hochkönig (9639 ft) is actually on Austrian ground, but their landmark, 'King Watzmann' (8904 ft) is one of the characteristic mountains of Bavaria. Its eastern rock face (5905 ft) – the highest wall in the Eastern Alps! – soars precipitously above that jewel of a lake, Königssee and the hurly-burly of the summer tourists who inundate this beauty spot. Johann Grill, commonly called Kederbacher, a mountain guide of Ramsau, traversed this huge precipice with Otto Schück of Vienna as long ago as 1881. Hochkalter, with its 'blue ice', the only German glacier and the northernmost one in the Alps, as well as the wide plateau of the Steinernes Meer (Stony Ocean) must be mentioned; the latter is a paradise for the touring skier – but only one of the many mountains in the alpine world surrounding the market town of Berchtesgaden. At its foot lie Salzburg and Bad Reichenhall, both on the north side.

The Tennen Mountains and the Dachstein Group have enormous caverns inside them. On the Hohen Dachstein (9829 ft) we find the last glaciation, the last elevation up to almost 3000 metre-level in the North Limestone Alps. The Wall of the Dachstein South Face and the crags of the Gosau Crest attract rock-climbers from Munich to Vienna. It is only a matter of time before a connection between the north side (Obertraun-Krippenstein) and the south side (Ramsau-Hunerkogel) by cable railway will be established. On the question of the South Face Railway, the interests of tourism have already outmanoevred the efforts of protestors from all over the world who favour the preservation of natural amenities.

Further to the east, the mountains become lower and lower until they decline into the rolling hills of the Viennese Forest. Of the ten groups between the much frequented holiday land of the Salzkammergut and Vienna, the following still have considerable importance to the mountaineer or the skier: the enormous plateau of the Totes Gebirg (Hoher Priel, 8284 ft); the Enns Valley Alps (or Gesäuse; Hochtor, 7782 ft) as a Viennese rock-climbers' paradise above the Enns break-through and finally, Rax and Schneeberg, these being on Vienna's doorstep. These last two groups rank before the Semmering, over which the Semmering Railway runs connecting Vienna with Styria since 1848.

*

The smallest alpine country, the Duchy of Liechtenstein, forms the western edge of the Rhätikons and thus of the Central Alps; the frontier between Switzerland and Vorarlberg runs along the main ridge of this group and over its highest mountain, the Scesaplana (9741 ft). The "Montafon Ski Stadium" stands in high esteem among skiers as do the South Walls between Drusenfluh and Sulzfluh among rock-climbers. The Silvretta, which follows the Rhätikons immediately, shows quite a different landscape owing to the extensive glaciation. Here all the mountain cabins are overcrowded in spring. The highest peak of the Silvretta, Piz Linard (11,201 ft) stands wholly on Swiss ground and dominates the Lower Engadine, for on the Dreiländer Spitze, three states meet, viz., Grisons, Tyrol and Vorarlberg. The skiing slopes of Motto-Naluns above Schuls (Scuol) are part of the Silvretta Group, but not those on the Idalpe, to which the 'Silvretta Railway' runs from Ischgl. Here we find ourselves already in the smaller Samnaun Group (Muttler, 10,810 ft) where the customs-free area in the Samnaun Valley is widely known. This peculiarity goes back to the days when this high Swiss valley could only be reached by passing over Austrian territory. Today a narrow little road leads up from the Inn Valley Road. I once even saw a car with a large boat-trailer blocking the traffic there; its driver certainly only wished to avail himself of the opportunity to buy petrol and other things cheaply. Beyond the Paznaun Valley, from which the Silvretta High-Alpine Road runs into Montafon, the Fervall Group (Kuchen Spitze, 10,400 ft) completes this block of mountains between Rhine, Inn and Arlberg.

In the Eastern Alps, the greatest area of glaciation is found in the Ötztal Alps, which fill the land between Reschen and Timmelsjoch and from Inn to Etsch. Here, as in the Stubai Alps, the eastern continuation (as far as the Brenner Pass), the Austro-Italian frontier runs along

their main crests. From the north, the valleys of the Kauner, Pitz, Ötz, Sellrain and Stubai run down from the heights and they have ensured sharp divisions into side ridges. Both mountain groups have great interest for the climbers and the skiers, the chief downhill runs being in Sölden and Obergurgl in the Ötz Valley while Vent as well as Fulpmes and Neustift over in the Stubai district are old haunts of the climbers. The extensive, ridged plateaux of these two groups which, alone on the North Tyrol side and including the frontier peak, can boast of 256 summits over 3000 metres high in the Ötztal Group and 151 in the Stubai district have too much to offer; Wild Spitze (12,384 ft) and Weißkugel (12,291 ft) in the former and Zuckerhütl (11,506 ft) and Schrankogel (11,467 ft) in the latter are all we have space to name. In the Kauner Ridge, between the Pitz and Kauner Valleys, as also in the Kalkkögel, there are difficult crags to climb. This is wedge of limestone inserted in the original rocks of the Central Alps and lies above the Olympic slopes of Axamer Lizum and above the Stubai Valley. Southern outliers of these immense mountain systems appear as separate groups in the southeast, the Sarntal Alps, a quiet district for walkers between Bozen and Sterzing and Meran and Brixen as well as the south-westerly Sesvenna Group. Piz Sesvenna and Piz Lischana dominate the triangle of three states between the Reschen and Ofen Passes in which the greater part of the Swiss National Park is situated.

East of the most important East-Alpine pass, that used by the railway and, in the near future, the "autobahn", viz., the Brenner Pass (4511 ft) lie the Zillertal Alps (Hochfeiler, 11,558 ft) and its northern outlier—a joy to skiers—the Tux Alps. Mountain railwys and lifts in the Ziller Valley (Mayrhofen), in the Tux and Gerlos Valleys as well as up Patscherkofel, long famous for skiing, and Glungezer are attracting increasing numbers of skiers. In this respect, the Tux and Zillertal Alps are, however, surpassed by the Kitzbühl Alps, where the humming of lifts is heard on almost all the gentle slopes of these slate mountains. Kitzbühl itself and Saalbach in the Glemm Valley are winter-sports centres of international standing; Zell am See with Schmittenhöhe, Kirchberg, Hopfgarten, Alpbach and the Wildschönau as well as many smaller places in the group, divided into two by the road over Thun Pass, allow people of even limited means to have a share of the joys of skiing.

Without noticeable break, the Alps of the Zillertal join the much divided system of the Hohe Tauern; these are exceeded in length alone by the Niedere (Lower) Tauern further east. The chief peaks of the Hohe Tauern are encircled by wide capes of glaciers once more; the Pasterze is the largest glacier in the Eastern Alps even and lies between the highest peak in Austria, the Gross Glockner (12,461 ft) and the motley scene on the Franz Josef Height, the terminus of the Glacier Road, a side road from the Gross Glockner High-Alpine Road. Besides this main road, opened in 1935 and rising to an altitude of 8225 ft between Bruck in Pinzgau and Heiligenblut, the Hohe Tauern are crossed by the new Felbertauern Road between Mittersill and East Tyrol but through a 3.25-mile tunnel as well as by the 5.3-mile railway tunnel driven through the Hohe Tauern between Mallnitz in Carinthia and the Gastein Valley, as long ago as in 1908. The road over the Radstadt Tauern, resulting in the development of the new, first-class winter-sports centre at Obertauern, and that over the Rottenmann Tauern lead over the Niedere Tauern. A dignitary of the Church, the Bishop-Prince of Gurk, Altgraf Salm-Reifferscheid ordered the ascent of the Gross Glockner towards the end of the 18th century. Supporting bases were established in 1799, a cross was set up on the lower peak, Klein Glockner, and in 1800, the high summit was reached. As early as in 1876, the Margrave Alfred Pallavicini of Vienna together with three guides climbed up an ice couloir, now named after him, to the saddle between Klein and Gross Glockner, on which occasion the guide Josef Tribusser is said to have cut 2500 steps in the ice alone. The "immemorial majesty" of the Gross Venedig Peak (12,054 ft) was assaulted by Archduke Johann in 1828 – but in vain; not before 1841 did an entire expedition, under the leadership of J. v. Kürsinger, a Mittersill administrator, conquer its glacial cap, which is visible

from as far away as the Bavarian Plateau. A new era of ice techniques began in 1924, when the Munich Surveyor of Works, Dr. Willo Welzenbach first used ice pitons while making the first ascent of the North-West Face of Gr. Wiesbachhorn.

At the foot of this rocky mountain-side, in the Kaprun Valley, today we find immense dam-constructions (Moserboden and Limberg Dams) and a cable railway to a height of over 9850 ft, which facilitates the summer skiing on the Gross Kitzsteinhorn. Included in the Hohe Tauern there are, besides the Venediger and Glockner Groups, the Granatspitze Group, lying between them, with Gr. Muntanitz (10,600 ft); further east the Goldberg Group with Hocharn (10,665 ft) and the Ankogel Group (Hochalm Spitze, 11,007 ft) as well as the southern outliers, the Rieserfern Group with the mighty Hochgall (11,285 ft), the Villgraten Mountains on the ridge forming the frontier between East and South Tyrol, and the Schober and Kreuzeck Groups. The Niedere Tauern culminate in Hochgolling (9393 ft). In the Noric and Cetic Alps, the Central Alps come to their eastern end.

*

For the last time we set out to make our way from west to east and this time through the Southern East Alps. East of the Bernina, Livigno and Bergamo Alps, we come to two extensive glacial regions and to immense mountains, the Ortler Group between Vinschgau and Sulzberg Valley, as well as the mountain groups south of this and named after their two chief peaks, Adamello (11,660 ft) and Presanella (11,667 ft). "King Ortler" (12,792 ft) and Königs Spitze (12,661 ft) above Sulden and Trafoi, which used to be South Tyrolese mountaineers' villages but are now winter-sports centres, of course – and these peaks are among the highest and finest in the Eastern Alps; Cevedale (12,366 ft) is one of the highest frequented by skiers anywhere in the Alps. Like many other high peaks, the Ortler was also climbed by order of an exalted personage; Archduke Johann issued the order and the "Passeirer Josele" – the chamois hunter, Josef Pichler – found the way up, on September 27th,

1804. On the glaciers of the Ortler and the Adamello Groups, just as in the pathless rocky landscape of the Dolomites and the Carnic Alps, a bitter high-alpine war was waged from 1915 to 1918, the traces of which are still met with by the mountaineer in these regions. Strategic reasons were also decisive for the construction of the Stilfserjoch Road. This road, it is true, is closed in winter, it being the highest crossing over the Eastern Alps (9045 ft), but from early summer on, high, summer skiing grounds are alive with skiers carried up by constant streams of chair-lifts.

The Nonsberg Alps extending in a long north to south line exercise a considerable attraction on tourists by reason of the craggy mountains of the Brenta in their south-west corner; Madonna di Campiglio is the main centre, Cima Tosa (10,420 ft) their highest and Campanile Basso ("Guglia di Brenta") their best-known peak. Climbers frequently count the Brenta, based on dolomite rock, as one of the Dolomite Group but these two groups are separated by the wide valley of the Etsch and by the Fleimstal Alps, a comparatively little visited mountain region. The true Dolomites occupy the large area between the Puster Valley in the north and the Eggen Valley and Rolle Pass, in the south. In the west, they are bordered by the Eisack while in the east they merge into the Bellunese Alps. South of Trento, the Brenta and the Fleimstal Alps, the Lake Garda and the Brescian Groups as well as, east of the Etsch, the Vincentine Alps lose both height and importance as they approach the fringe of the Alps.

The much sub-divided Dolomites cannot be covered in a few lines. Their highest mountain is also the one with the most aspects: from the north it is the Marmolada (10,965 ft), a grand mountain for skiers, accessible by railway and by lift, while the precipitous front of its broad South Wall is the preserve of the expert rock-climber. "Il regno del sesto grado" (a realm of Grade VI difficulties) is the Italian phrase applied to the Civetta; the English is "hard very severe". But it caused a greater sensation when the North Wall of the Drei Zinnen was climbed by various cragsman's paths; the ascents by the Munich men, Solleder and Lettenbauer in 1925 across the Civetta North-West Wall and by the Italians, Comici and the Dimai brothers, via the North Face of the Drei Zinnen in 1931, introduced a new epoch in the sport of rock-climbing. The Rosengarten with the pinnacled Vajolettürmen looks down into the streets of Bozen. The most hazardous of these pinnacles, the Winklerturm was first climbed solo by a 17-year-old boy from a Munich grammar school, Georg Winkler, in 1887. Cortino d'Ampezzo, below the Tofanen, was once the scene of the Olympic Games and is now the centre for the eastern Dolomites. Lanfkofel and Sella rising above the Grödner Valley (the arena for the World Championships held in 1970), the Sexten Mountains in the north and, not least among these mountains, the "wild beauty" Pala above San Martino di Castrozza—these can only give some indication of the magical world of the Dolomites—but their beauties have by no means been exhausted. The magnificent roads that cross over the great Dolomite passes (Grödner, Sella-Pordoijoch, Falzarego Passes etc.) have made of these once impassable mountains a land for tourists and holiday-makers such as can scarcely be equalled anywhere in the Alps. Skiing, too, has come to these rocky mountains to stay.

Not much smaller than the Dolomites, but less opened up and that at only a few places—for instance, "the most illogical Alpine mountain", the Campanile di Val Montanaia, popular with climbers there are the Carnic Alps which run beyond the Piave to the east. In its chief crest, along which the Austro-Italian frontier runs, we find its highest mountains (Hohe Warte, 9144 ft) and also the greatest number of mountain cabins. The roads through the German-speaking enclave, Sappada and further south, over the Mauria Pass, cross the southern section of this group in an east to west direction.

Parallel to the frontier ridge, the long chain of the Gailtal Alps runs between the Gail and the Drau rivers; it extends from the fine climbers' mountains of the "Lienz Dolomites" via the East-Tyrol capital, Lienz, to the Dobratsch above Villach, a mountain long renowned for its splendid views.

We have now arrived at the eastern end of the Southern Alps also, in the vicinity of the point where the frontiers of Austria, Italy and Jugoslavia meet. Only the last three groups have still to be accounted for: the Karawanken, which separate Slovenia and Carinthia, their highest peak being Hochstuhl (7346 ft); the Steiner Alps (Grintovec, 8392 ft) which, except for quite a small triangle jutting into this group and attracting attention as the southern-most tip of Austria, are entirely in Jugoslavia, and finally the Julian Alps. These last represent the most important mountains of Jugoslavia in respect of tourism, but about one third of the group belongs to Italy. This Italian part dominated by the Wischberg (8767 ft) and Montasch (9029 ft) is still comparatively unfrequented while the Slovenes have given all their enthusiasm and love to this, their highest mountain range. They have opened up this lovely alpine world to the limit—and sometimes almost beyond! In the middle of difficult rock-faces, exercising great technical skill, they have made steps for the intrepid climber. The numerous mountain cabins belonging to the Slovenian Alpine Club (Planinska zveza Slovenije), established in 1893, offer hospitality to all mountaineers. The great developer of the Julian Alps, an Austrian resident of Triest, Dr. Julius Kugy (1858–1944), is equally honoured by alpinists of all three countries that meet in this region. His Memorial stands in Trenta, in the heart of the Slovenian part of the Julian Alps, not far from their highest mountain, Triglav (9396 ft). On the summit commanding magnificent views, rock-climbers who traverse its North Wall (4921 ft) meet countless other alpinists who have come up, from four high-lying hostels, on paths made safe for them. The valleys of the Wochein Save and the Isonzo (Soča) lead into the mountains, the more interesting roads cross over the Vršič and Predil Passes. The high-lights of the Julian Alps include Lake Wochein and Lake Bled (Veldes) as well as the pearl bracelet of the seven Triglav Lakes. The heights of the Komna offer fine skiing grounds; on the ski-jumping hill at Planica, the 100 metre mark was first exceeded in 1936, in a ski-flight.

*

We have now completed a round 750-mile journey through the Alps from Nice on the Côte d'Azur to Laibach at the foot of the Steiner Alps. However varied the impressions may have been, the final assessment must be

"No lovelier country-side …"

LES ALPES

Alpes, vous me resterez
inoubliables à jamais

Nikolaus Lenau, 1802—1850

«The Playground of Europe»

Titre d'un ouvrage par
Leslie Stephen, 1871

Lieu enchanté pour l'âme du poète — emplacement sportif pour l'alpiniste. Entre ces deux extrêmes, nous trouvons de nombreuses possibilités de considérer les Alpes.

Le géographe, le géologue, le minéralogiste, le glaciologue et nombre d'autres savants y ont toujours trouvé de quoi procéder à des recherches, à des subdivisions; elles leur offrent l'occasion d'émettre des théories — qui ont entraîné des théories contraires — et d'écrire des livres.

Autrefois, l'importance des Alpes résidait dans leurs richesses naturelles, minerais, sel, bois. Aujourd'hui, elles sont devenues l'un des principaux lieux de villégiature d'Europe. Le tourisme est désormais un facteur décisif pour les pays sur lesquels s'étend la chaîne des Alpes; il a d'ailleurs vu sa signification doubler depuis que le ski connaît une telle popularité.

Jadis, les Alpes constituaient pour la circulation le plus grand handicap existant sur le continent. Et les techniciens de se mettre à l'œuvre: les romains ont aménagé les premières routes de cols et, depuis le milieu du XIXe siècle, les Alpes sont traversées par des voies ferrées. Les tunnels sont de plus en plus longs, et la technique la plus récente est celle des téléphériques.

Bergers, pâtres et chasseurs furent sans doute les premiers à pénétrer dans les zones élevées de la montagne. Ils n'y restèrent pas longtemps seuls. Les intellectuels sont venus à leur tour. C'étaient des chercheurs — et parfois des hommes qui se donnaient pour tels quand la curiosité était leur seul mobile. Puis un rapport nouveau s'établit entre l'homme et la nature; la curiosité était désormais légitime et l'alpinisme devenait un mouvement de masse.

Ce mouvement de masse était si considérable qu'il ne se manifestait pas uniquement dans les pays alpins proprement dits. Ce n'est pas par hasard que le premier club alpin a été créé à Londres (Alpine Club, 1857); en effet, les alpinistes anglais ont largement contribué — sous la conduite de guides locaux — à la découverte systématique des Alpes, notamment des Alpes Occidentales. Peu à peu, les pays alpins ont, eux aussi, créé leurs clubs. En 1862 fut créé le Club Alpin Autrichien (Österreichischer Alpenverein, ÖVA); en 1863, le Club Alpin Suisse (Schweizer Alpenclub, SAC); la même année, le Club Alpin Italien (Club Alpino Italiano, CAI); en 1869, le Club Alpin Allemand (Deutscher Alpenverein, DAV) et en 1874 le Club Alpin Français (CAF). De 1874 à 1945, DAV et ÖAV étaient réunis et constituaient le Club Alpin Allemand et Autrichien (DÖAV). Tous les pays, si plats soint-ils, possèdent aujourd'hui des associations d'alpinisme. Elles s'appellent «Club Alpin» même dans les pays fort éloignés des Alpes tels que l'Australie, la Japon ou les Etats-Unis. Les clubs d'une même catégorie étant désireux d'être dirigés par une organisation suprême, les associations d'alpinisme d'Europe et des autres continents et, pour des motifs politiques, de l'Est et de l'Ouest, se sont réunies pour former l'Union Internationale des Associations d'Alpinisme.

Ce mouvement de masse a également favorisé certains domaines artistiques; il entraîna une littérature abondante concernant les Alpes et la peinture elle-même y a trouvé de nouveaux thèmes. Avant sa destruction quasi totale lors d'un bombardement en 1943, la bibliothèque du Club Alpin Allemand à Munich était, avec ses 60.000 volumes, la plus grande bibliothèque spécialisée qui soit. Aujourd'hui, elle possède environ 24.000 volumes et 2.000 cartes; elle collectionne en outre quelque 250 périodiques consacrés à ce domaine.

*

«La zone de haute montagne des Alpes donne à l'Europe son caractère particulier et noble. L'influence de la montagne se manifeste sur une partie considérable de ce continent ... Les Alpes refroidissent certes l'Europe Centrale; en contrepartie, elles lui donnent la grandeur majestueuse de leurs formes, leurs eaux abondantes qui s'écoulent à travers les pays limitrophes, leur fraîcheur et leur beauté. Les Alpes, c'est la couronne de l'Europe, couronne dont les joyaux étincellent sur leurs glaciers.»

C'est en ces termes poétiques que H. Beitzke, capitaine de l'armée prussienne et géographe, commençait son ouvrage de 902 pages, «Les Alpes» (Colberg, 1843). Beaucoup plus prosaïque, le dictionnaire nous dit: «Les Alpes, chaîne de montagne la plus élevée d'Europe; elles s'étendent entre le 43e et le 48e degré de latitude et le 5e et le 16e degré de longitude. Dessinant dans leur ensemble un arc immense, elles s'étirent du Golfe de Gênes jusqu'à Vienne et au Karst. Le Col d'Altare (459 m) constitue la limite entre les Alpes et l'Apennin ... Leur longueur est d'environ 1.300 kilomètres, leur largeur varie entre 150 et 200 kilomètres ... Les Alpes couvrent une superficie de 220.000 kilomètres carrés.» (Brockhaus, Encyclopédie, 1967.)

Des siècles ont été nécessaires pour permettre d'en arriver à cette connaissance des Alpes. Les géographes de l'antiquité étaient loin de savoir l'étendue, même approximative, de cette chaîne montagneuses. En 1574, on trouve encore dans un ouvrage du Suisse Josias Simler intitulé «De alpibus commentarius» et que l'on peut considérer comme le premier livre important sur les Alpes: «Nous partageons l'opinion des auteurs de jadis qui disaient: Les Alpes proprement dites sont la chaîne de montagne qui limite l'Italie.» Soit dit en passant, le chapitre XIV de ce livre traite «les difficultés des voies alpines et la manière d'en venir à bout»; c'est donc pour ainsi dire le premier manuel d'alpinisme.

Les recherches et études effectuées jusqu'à maintenant ont permis d'obtenir des Alpes une connaissance assez exacte; un point reste toutefois litigieux, à savoir la subdivision de cette chaîne montagneuse. On avait tout d'abord adopté la division suivante en trois parties: les Alpes franco-italiennes ou Occidentales, les Alpes suisses ou Alpes Centrales et les Alpes Orientales. Une nouvelle théorie s'est imposée peu à peu, la division en Alpes Occidentales et Alpes Orientales. Les savants sont relativement d'accord quant à la limite séparant les deux zones; elle passe au Col de Splügen (Rhin, Rhin postérieur, Splügen, Liro,

28

Mera, Lac de Côme). Toutefois, cette division va à l'encontre du sentiment de nombreux écrivains; pour ces derniers, Bernina et Bergell «appartiennent aux Alpes Occidentales car leur paysage manifeste les caractères typiques de cette partie des Alpes» (K. Lugan, «Les Alpes Orientales, 1969). Ces écrivains géographes oublient sans doute qu'un déplacement de la limite vers l'est — à peu près au niveau de la frontière suisse — entraînerait un manque de séparation naturelle. Bernina et Bergell mis à part, cinq massifs dépourvus de tout caractère commun avec les Alpes Occidentales (Alpes de Plessur, Oberhalbstein, Albula, Livigno et massif de Bergame) seraient alors classés dans cette zone.

Effectuons donc un voyage dans les Alpes, de la Méditerranée au Danube. Nous allons considérer les principaux massifs, les sommets intéressants, les localités importantes, les artères principales et les événements capitaux de l'histoire des Alpes. Ce faisant, la division de la chaîne nous servira pour ainsi dire de guide. Il est bien impossible de décrire tous les massifs; cela dépasserait d'ailleurs de beaucoup le cadre de la préface d'un ouvrage illustré consacré aux Alpes. Nous ne nous attarderons pas non plus sur des questions géologiques ou autres de nature analogue — au risque de faire naître l'impression d'une lacune de culture générale.

Les Alpes Occidentales

Au-dessus des plages, promenades, casinos et marchés de la Côte d'Azur et de la Riviera s'élèvent les *Alpes Niçoises* et les *Alpes Liguriennes*. Ces dernières atteignent déjà l'altitude respectable de 3.297 mètres (Punta Argentera). Sur le versant français, c'est là que se trouvent les stations de sports d'hiver les plus méridionales, Auron et Valberg. Ces centres n'étant qu'à environ 90 kilomètres de Nice, on peut, par une belle journée de printemps, faire du ski dans les Alpes puis du ski nautique sur la Méditerranée.

Ce massif se continue vers l'ouest par les *Alpes de Provence*, massif calcaire sans caractère de haute montagne.

On y découvre les gorges du Verdon, les plus imposantes d'Europe; du haut du Mont Ventoux (1.912 m), on peut admirer un panorama magnifique. C'est d'ailleurs au Mont Ventoux qu'a commencé l'histoire de l'alpinisme dans les Alpes. Francesco Petrarca, poète célèbre sous le nom de Pétrarque, en fit l'ascension avec son frère le 26 avril 1336; puis il écrivit au cardinal Colonna: «J'ai fait l'ascension du plus haut sommet de la région dont le nom est fort justifié; je m'y suis rendu dans le seul but de connaître la hauteur notable de l'endroit.» Il avoue sans détour qu'il a été poussé par cette passion qui est à l'origine de tous les actes de l'histoire alpine: «Cette montagne visible de loin s'élevait continuellement devant mes yeux; finalement, je n'ai pu résister à mon désir.»

Plus au nord, on se trouve confronté avec un bloc gigantesque dont les sommets dépassent 4.000 mètres; ce sont les *Alpes Cottiennes* et les *Alpes du Dauphiné*. Les portes de ces massifs importants sont Grenoble à l'ouest et Turin à l'est. France et Italie sont reliées par la ligne ferroviaire qui porte le nom du Mont Cenis mais qui emprunte effectivement un tunnel de 12 kilomètres au Col de Fréjus. La route, elle, passe au Col du Mont Cenis (2.084 m), entre Susa et Lanslebourg; une autre utilise le col du Montgenèvre (entre Susa et Briançon). Les automobilistes amateurs de routes de cols peuvent se procurer un guide leur indiquant nombre de cols intéressants dans les Alpes françaises (direction Nord-Sud). La célèbre route des Alpes traverse à elle seule dix cols entre Thonon-les-Bains (sur le Lac Léman) et Nice; parmi ces cols, six sont à plus de 2.000 mètres et le plus élevé est le col de l'Iseran (2.770 m). Plus à l'ouest, une autre route également célèbre et belle — la Route Napoléon — conduit de Grenoble à Cannes.

Le massif des *Alpes Cottiennes* doit son nom à Cottius, jadis roi des tribus liguriennes. Ce massif possède un seul sommet et une seule localité célèbres, le Monte Viso et Sestrière. C'est au pied du Monte Viso (3.843 m), «le sommet le plus isolé des Alpes et qui, de ce fait, domine le mieux ses environs» (Umlauft), que jaillit le Pô. Bien que la première ascension ait été réalisée en 1861 par des Anglais accompagnés d'un guide français, le Monte Viso n'en reste pas moins la montagne italienne par excellence. C'est au sommet de cette montagne que le ministre Quintino Sella et ses amis ont décidé en 1863 la création du Club Alpin Italien. En 1931 a commencé l'aménagement de Sestrière, premier centre de sports d'hiver né de toutes pièces sur le papier à l'instigation du Sénateur Agnelli, chef des Usines Fiat.

Au-delà de la frontière se dressent majestueux les sommets des *Alpes du Dauphiné*. Là aussi on trouve des centres de sports d'hiver «à l'automatisation parfaite» tels que l'Alpe d'Huez, les Deux Alpes et Chamrousse. Toutefois, le Dauphiné reste le paradis des alpinistes. Les deux principaux centres sont deux petites localités: La Grave au pied du col du Lautaret et La Bérarde dans la vallée du Vénéon. Entre ces deux villages s'élève la Meije (3.983 m), massif imposant composé de plusieurs sommets. Les alpinistes avaient déjà fait l'ascension de tous les sommets importants des Alpes; seule la Meije restait invaincue. L'exploit de la première ascension a été accompli par Boileau de Castelnau, son père et son fils Gaspard. Puis les Autrichiens Ludwig Purtscheller et Emil et Otto Zsigmondy ont réalisé en 1885 l'ascension complète; ce fait est également entré dans les annales de l'alpinisme, d'autant plus que ces trois hommes l'ont accompli seuls à une époque où tous les alpinistes étaient accompagnés d'une guide. Quelques jours plus tard, le Dr. Emil Zsigmondy, auteur d'un manuel d'alpinisme, a trouvé la mort au cours d'une tentative d'ascension du versant sud de la Meije. Le sommet le plus élevé de ce massif, la Barre des Ecrins (4.101 m) est à la fois le quatre mille le plus méridional des la chaîne des Alpes. Edward Whymper, spécialiste du massif du Matterhorn, en fit l'ascension en 1864.

A l'écart de la haute montagne proprement dite s'élève dans le Dauphiné un pic bizarre, le Mont Aiguille (2.097 m); n'ayant que des parois rocheuses, il était jadis considéré comme invincible. Un jour, le roi Charles VIII a ordonné son ascension; et son valet de chambre Antoine de Ville de partir à l'assaut le 25 juin 1492. Accompagné de plusieurs hommes munis de cordes et d'échelles, il entreprit l'escalade de la paroi abrupte haute de 300 m.

Après quoi Monsieur de Ville écrivit sur place ses impressions sur «le chemin le plus terrible et le plus épouvantable qui soit». Ce compte-rendu est à considérer comme l'ancêtre des récits actuels.

Avant de quitter la direction sud-nord pour s'orienter d'ouest en est, la chaîne se rétrécit dans le massif des *Alpes Graies*. La route emprunte le col du Petit St-Bernard (2.188 m) pour relier Val d'Isère et Val d'Aoste. Au milieu du Parc National Italien, zone de protection de la faune et de la flore et, ici, particulièrement du bouquetin, s'élève le principal sommet du massif, le Grand Paradis (4.061 m). Sur le versant français sont situés des centres de sports d'hiver jouissant d'une renommée mondiale. Les skieurs dignes de ce nom se doivent d'avoir effectué les descentes de Val d'Isère et de Courcheval.

Au-delà du Val d'Aoste, les Alpes atteignent leur altitude maxima. Autour du majestueux Mont Blanc (4.807 m), les *Alpes de Savoie* groupent une bonne douzaine de quatre mille et quantité d'autres sommets parmi lesquels se dressent de nombreuses «aiguilles». Chamonix et Courmayeur, les deux principales localités de la région, sont reliées par la route grâce au tunnel du Mont-Blanc (11,6 km) et par un véritable réseau de téléphériques franchissant les glaciers. La plus haute montagne d'Europe est à la fois le premier grand sommet européen dont on ait réalisé l'ascension; le docteur Paccard, medecin à Chamonix, réalisa cet exploit avec Jacques Balmat le 8 août 1786; ils remportaient ainsi le prix décerné par le professeur genevois H. G. de Saussure. Accompagné de Balmat et d'autres alpinistes, Saussure atteignit lui-même le sommet le 3 août 1787. L'historiographie alpine considéra cette date — et non celle de la première ascension — comme la «naissance de l'alpinisme». Les descriptions des ascensions du Mont Blanc et des différents sommets de ce massif ont été réunies au prix d'efforts considérables; elles ont donné naissance à un ouvrage en trois volumes. Pas une paroi, pas une crête qui ait échappé aux alpinistes; la paroi nord des Grandes Jorasses possède même plusieurs «routes». La technique mettant au service de l'alpiniste du matériel de plus en plus perfectionné et la technique de l'escalade étant devenue de plus en plus parfaite, le mot «impossible» est pour ainsi dire banni du langage des alpinistes.

Entre les cols du Grand St-Bernard (2.473 m) et du Simplon (2.005 m), s'étendent les *Alpes Valaisannes*. Comme le précédent, ce massif fait la joie des alpinistes et des skieurs. De par ses dimensions et l'altitude de ses différents sommets, il dépasse même les Alpes de Savoie. Le groupe le plus élevé, celui du Mont Rose (Pointe Dufour, 4.634 m), se compose d'une couronne de sommets. Mais, qui dit Alpes Valaisannes pense Matterhorn (4.477 m). Films et romans ont fait revivre l'histoire dramatique de la première ascension et contribué ainsi à la popularité de cette gigantesque pyramide qui s'élève entre Zermatt et Breuil; cette localité s'appelle d'ailleurs maintenant Cervinia, d'après la montagne proche, le Mont Cervin. Cette histoire est la suivante: deux cordées rivales, l'une menée par l'Anglais Edward Whymper, l'autre par le guide italien Jean-Antoine Carrel étaient parties simultanément à l'assaut du sommet. Le 14 juillet 1865, la cordée de Whymper atteignait le sommet alors que celle de Carrel, partie de Breuil, en était toute proche. Puis, lors de la descente, ce fut la catastrophe; quatre des sept alpinistes ont trouvé la mort. Le Matterhorn a de nouveau fait parler de lui en 1931 quand les deux Munichois Franz et Toni Schmid réalisèrent l'ascension de la paroi nord; à court d'argent, ils étaient venus en Suisse à bicyclette. A cette occasion, le Comité Olympique a décerné pour la première fois en 1932 des médailles d'or d'alpinisme. Malheureusement, Toni Schmid n'a plus connu cet honneur. Zermatt, Saas-Fee et Cervinia comptent parmi les grands centres alpins de ski. Téléphériques et remonte-pentes dépassent déjà la limite des trois mille mètres; de nouveaux buts sont déjà fixés: Kleines Matterhorn (3.883 m) à partir de Zermatt; Feekopf (3.888 m) à partir de Saas-Fee; avec son téléphérique de l'Aiguille du Midi (3.842 m), Chamonix doit être dépassé doublement!

Faisant suite aux Alpes Valaisannes, nous trouvons les *Alpes Lépontiennes* (Monte Leone, 3.558 m) et le *massif de l'Adula* (Rheinwaldhorn, 3.046 m). A Splügen, on arrive à la limite entre Alpes Occidentales et Alpes Orientales. Parallèles à ces groupes, nous avons au-delà de la vallée du Rhône le *massif du Chablais* avec le Dent du Midi (3.260 m), les *Alpes Fribourgeoises* (Wildhorn, 3.248 m), les *Alpes Bernoises* et les *Alpes de Glaris* (Tödi, 3.623 m). Le col de la Furka et le col de l'Oberalp permettent de passer facilement de la vallée du Rhin à celle du Rhône et vice versa. Dans la direction nord-sud, le lac des Quatre-Cantons et le Tessin sont réunis par la route et par la voie ferrée qui empruntent respectivement le col et le tunnel du St-Gothard (2.112 m). Plus à l'ouest, la ligne ferroviaire Lötschberg-Simplon traverse deux tunnels sur le trajet Kandersteg — Brigue — Domodossola. Le col de Grimsel (2.165 m) qui permet de passer de l'Oberland bernois à la vallée supérieure du Rhône n'est ouvert qu'en été. Inauguré en 1967, le tunnel de San Bernardino décharge considérablement le col de Splügen qui devait auparavant absorber toute la circulation se dirigeant de la région du Rhin postérieur vers les lacs d'Italie du nord.

De par leur altitude, leurs glaciers et leur importance touristique, les *Alpes Bernoises* occupent la première place dans la partie septentrionale des Alpes suisses. Elles contiennent neuf quatre mille dont le principal est le Finsteraarhorn (4.273 m); c'est là que s'étend le plus grand glacier des Alpes, l'Aletschgletscher (115 km²). Visible depuis Berne et dominant des centres de sports d'hiver célèbres — Grindelwald, Wengen, Mürren — se dresse le groupe des trois sommets les plus célèbres des Alpes: Eiger, Mönch et Jungfrau. Grâce à la technique, on peut atteindre sans peine le Jungfraujoch (3.454 m). De là, l'ascension de la Jungfrau (4.158 m) et du Mönch (4.099m) ne cause pas de trop grandes difficultés aux alpinistes expérimentés. La paroi nord de l'Eiger, paroi meurtrière s'il en est, exerce, elle, une fascination étrange sur les «extrêmes» du monde entier. De 1935 à 1969, elle a coûté la vie à 35 alpinistes. 200 alpinistes ont escaladé cette paroi depuis sa première ascension par Heckmair, Vörg, Harrer et Kasparek en 1938; elle a été vaincue pour la première fois en hiver en 1961 et suivant la direttissima en 1966. En 1969, une cordée japonaise a réalisé pour la première fois la direttissima en été. Cette paroi a toujours offert de quoi satisfaire les amateurs de sensation: accidents et sauvetages spectaculaires, ascension du premier alpiniste solitaire (1963) et première ascension par une femme (1964), etc.

Nous sommes arrivés maintenant à la limite des Alpes Occidentales; avant de les quitter, citons encore Engelberg et son funiculaire conduisant au Titlis; le Mont Pilate et le Mont Rigi, deux sommets célèbres pour leur magnifique panorama; les cantons primitifs de la Suisse, lieu où Friedrich Schiller a placé l'action de son «Guillaume Tell»; Santis et Alpstein; les Kreuzberge à l'ouest du lac de Constance; les Churfirsten au bord du Walensee; le Piz Sol, montagne idéale pour le ski; la vallée du Rhin et Flims, célèbre centre de sports d'hivers.

Les Alpes Orientales

Nous avons passé le Rhin mais nous restons encore en Suisse. De Coire, chef-lieu du Canton des Grisons, on gagne la Haute Engadine par la route via Lenzerheide, Oberhalbstein et le col du Julier; la voie ferrée, elle, emprunte le tunnel de l'Albula. Le nom *«massif de Plessur»* est peu connu; par contre, les centres de sports d'hiver de cette région — Arosa, Davos — jouissent d'une renommée mondiale. La région des *Alpes Rhétiques* (Piz Platta, 3398 m; Piz Kesch, 3.420 m) entre le col du Julier et le col de la Flüela ne connaît pas encore les grandes foules sur les pistes. Par contre, alpinistes et skieurs amateurs d'excursions apprécient cette région entre Davos et St-Moritz.

Au sud de St-Moritz et de Pontresina, entre le col de la Maloja (1.815 m) et celui de la Bernina (2.323 m), s'élève le *massif de la Bernina*; c'est là que passe la frontière entre la Suisse et l'Italie. Le Piz Bernina (4.049 m) est le seul quatre mille des Alpes Orientales. Le Suisse Johann Coaz en fit la première ascension en 1850. La plus belle route conduisant au sommet a été explorée en 1878 par un Berlinois, le Dr. Paul Güssfeldt, accompagné de deux guides locaux. Alpinistes et skieurs amateurs d'excursions apprécient particulièrement le Piz Palu (3.905 m) tandis

que ceux qui préfèrent la descente séjournent dans la zone de téléphériques de la Diavolezza et du Piz Corvatsch, deux sommets offrant un panorama splendide. De Soglio — où a peint jadis Segantini et où les touristes tournent des kilomètres de pellicule — on jouit d'une vue magnifique sur le groupe de Bergell dont les parois granitiques (Piz Badile et autres) sont très recherchées des alpinistes.

Le bloc des six groupes constituant l'ouest des Alpes Orientales se termine par le *massif de Livigno* (Cima di Piazzi, 3.439 m) et, plus au sud, par les *Alpes de Bergame* (Pizzo di Scais, 3.040 m) entre Sondrio et Bergame.

*

Si la division des Alpes en général est encore sujet à litige, celle des Alpes Orientales est un fait reconnu. Elle découle d'ailleurs automatiquement des formations géologiques; on distingue les Alpes Calcaires du Nord, les Alpes Centrales et les Alpes du Sud. Suivons donc ces trois zones d'est en ouest.

Les *Alpes Calcaires du Nord* comprennent la totalité des Alpes allemandes; ces dernières constituent en effet une bande étroite s'étirant le long de la frontière autrichienne, du lac de Constance au Königssee. A l'ouest, nous avons d'abord le groupe constitué par le *Bregenzer Wald et le Lechquellengebirge* (massif où le Lech prend sa source), les *monts de l'Allgäu* et les *Lechtaler Alpen*. Les Monts de l'Allgäu sont en général des versants assez abrupts mais herbeux où l'edelweiss pousse à foison; mais cette plante est sévèrement protégée! Au nord, les principaux centres de sports d'hiver se trouvent dans les régions d'Hindelang, d'Oberstdorf et du Kleines Walsertal (territoire autrichien, cette vallée dépend de la Bavière du point de vue économique). Au sud, ce sont les stations voisines du col de l'Arlberg; c'est là, notamment à St-Anton et St-Christoph, qu'est né le style moderne du ski alpin. La Parseierspitze (3.038 m) dans les Lechtaler Alpen est le seul trois mille des Alpes Calcaires du Nord. Dans l'Allgäu, le sommet le plus élevé n'est pas le célèbre Mädelegabel mais le Grosser Krottenkopf (2.657 m).

32

A l'est de la percée du Lech s'élèvent les *Monts de l'Ammergau* avec, à leur pied, les châteaux de Neuschwanstein et Linderhof; près de Linderhof, Oberammergau, localité célèbre pour ses représentations de la Passion. Situées à proximité de Munich, les *Préalpes de Bavière* offrent de quoi satisfaire les amateurs de ski: Lenggries et le Brauneck, la dépression du Tegernsee, la région du Spitzingsee, Bayrischzell avec le Sudelfeld et le Wendelstein. Ces groupes constituent en quelque sorte les avant-postes d'autres groupes plus élevés et beaucoup plus intéressants pour les alpinistes: *Massifs du Wetterstein*, des *Mieminger*, du *Karwendel* et du *Rofan*, ce dernier étant situé à l'est de l'Achensee. Le centre de sports d'hiver par excellence est naturellement Garmisch-Partenkirchen, localité où furent organisés les Jeux Olympiques d'hiver 1936. Les pentes environnantes sont sillonnées de mécanismes de remontée de toutes sortes; trois possibilités s'offrent de gagner le seul sommet de la Zugspitze (2.964 m), le plus haut sommet d'Allemagne. Mittenwald et Seefeld sont deux autres centres très cotés de cette région alpine. Au sud du Karwendel s'étend Innsbruck, capitale du Tyrol et station dont la popularité a encore augmenté du fait des Jeux Olympiques d'hiver 1964. Les ascensions importantes effectuées dans le massif du Wetterstein sont légion et il est impossible de s'y attarder. Dans le massif du Karwendel (Birkkarspitze, 2.756 m), montagne composée de roche friable, une immense muraille appelée «Laliderer Wände» attire tout particulièrement les alpinistes.

Très recherchés sont également les versants du *Kaisergebirge*, le plus petit groupe des Alpes Orientales; sa partie méridionale, le Wilder Kaiser, est difficilement accessible. Par contre, des sommets tels que Totenkirchl, Fleischbank et Predigtstuhl sont entrés dans l'histoire de l'alpinisme. C'est là et dans les Dolomites que la technique de l'ascalade a été perfectionnée et amenée à son niveau actuel.

Au-dessus de la dépression du Chiemsee s'élèvent les *Alpes du Chiemgau*. Elles offrent d'excellentes conditions de ski et de villégiature: Reit-im-Winkl (Winklmoosalm) et Ruhpolding, localité où le tourisme social fait fureur. Plus au sud se dressent les *Steinberge* (environs de Lofer et de Leogang); ces deux groupes conduisent vers le groupe le plus oriental d'Allemagne possédant un caractère de haute montagne, les *Alpes de Berchtesgaden*. Leur point culminant, le Hochkönig (2.938 m), est sur le territoire autrichien; par contre, le signe caractéristique du groupe est le «König Watzmann» (2.714 m). Sa paroi haute de 1.800 mètres (c'est la plus importante des Alpes Orientales) surplombe le Königssee, lac ravissant où les touristes s'abattent en essaims dès que vient l'été. Johann Grill, guide de Ramsau connu sous le nom de Kederbacher, accompagna en 1881 le Viennois Otto Schück dans cette paroi. Citons encore dans cette région le Hochkalter avec son glacier (Blaueis), le seul glacier allemand et le plus septentrional des Alpes, et le haut-plateau du «Steinernes Meer» (Mer de pierre), véritable paradis pour les skieurs amateurs d'excursions. Au pied du versant nord sont situées Bad Reichenhall et Salzbourg.

Tennengebirge et *massif du Dachstein* possèdent d'immenses grottes glaciaires. Le Hoher Dachstein (2.996 m) est le dernier sommet des Alpes Calcaires du Nord atteignant presque 3.000 mètres. Sa paroi sud et les crêtes rocheuses des environs de Gosau attirent les alpinistes de Munich à Vienne. La liaison par téléphérique du côté nord (Obertraun-Krippenstein) et du côté sud (Ramsau-Hunerkogel) n'est plus qu'une question de temps. Les intérêts touristiques ont déjà, pour le téléphérique du versant sud, étouffé les protestations véhémentes des organismes chargés de la protection de la nature et du paysage.

A mesure que l'on s'avance vers l'est, la montagne s'abaisse de plus en plus pour former, dans le Wiener Wald, un ravissant paysage de collines. Citons parmi les dix groupes situés entre le Salzkammergut et Vienne les principaux massifs intéressants pour les alpinistes et les skieurs. Ce sont notamment le haut-plateau du *Totengebirge* (Hoher Priel, 2.514 m), zone de prédilection des alpinistes viennois au-dessus de la percée de l'Enns; le groupe du *Hochschwab* où s'exercent les alpinistes de Styrie; *Raxalpe* et *Schneeberg* sont enfin deux sommets facilement accessibles pour les Viennois. Les deux derniers groupes dominent le col du Semmering; c'est là que passe depuis 1848 la «Semmeringbahn», voie ferrée reliant Vienne à la Styrie.

La principauté de Liechtenstein, le plus petit pays alpin, constitue la limite occidentale du Rätikon et, ce faisant, des *Alpes Centrales*. La crête principale de ce groupe et son point culminant, la Schesaplana (2.969 m), dessine la frontière entre la Suisse et le Vorarlberg. Montafon est un paradis pour les skieurs; quant aux versants sud entre Drusenfluh et Sulzfluh, ils font la joie des alpinistes. Les glaciers du *massif de la Silvretta* donnent à cet autre groupe un caractère bien différent. Le printemps venu, tous les chalets et refuges se remplissent. Le point culminant, le Piz Linard (3.414 m) s'élève entièrement sur le territoire suisse et domine la Basse-Engadine. A la «Dreiländerspitze» se rencontrent Grisons, Vorarlberg et Tyrol. Le centre de sports d'hiver Motta-Naluns appartient à la Silvretta; par contre, l'Idalpe, terminus de la «Silvretta-Bahn», appartient déjà au petit *groupe des Samnaun* (Muttler, 3.298 m). Une vallée de cette région est bien connue pour l'absence de droits de douane. Cette particularité remonte à une époque lointaine où cette vallée n'était accessible qu'à partir de la Suisse. Aujourd'hui, une petite route y conduit. J'y ai même vu une voiture remorquant un canot encombrer la route et gêner la circulation; sans doute le conducteur voulait-il profiter de l'occasion pour faire des emplettes et acheter de l'essence à bon compte.

De l'autre côté de la vallée de la Paznaun d'où la route conduit vers le val de Montafon, le *Ferwall* (Kuchenspitze, 3.170 m) termine ce bloc montagneux limité par le Rhin, l'Arlberg et l'Inn.

La zone glaciaire la plus importante des Alpes Centrales est située dans les *Ötztaler Alpen*. Ce groupe couvre l'espace limité par le col de Reschen et le Timmelsjoch, l'Inn et l'Adige. La frontière austro-italienne suit la crête de ces montagnes, de même d'ailleurs que dans le groupe suivant, les *Stubaier Alpen*. C'est une région riche en vallées transversales — Kaunertal, Pitztal, Ötztal, Sellraintal et Stubaital; la montagne est ainsi divisée en crêtes latérales. Ces deux massifs sont du plus grand intérêt pour les alpinistes et les skieurs. Sölden et Ober-

gurgel dans l'Ötztal offrent de magnifiques pistes de descente. Vent et, dans la Stubaital, Fulpmes et Neustift sont depuis longtemps des citadelles de l'alpinisme. Les sommets sont non seulement nombreux mais aussi élevés. Les Ötztaler Alpen comptent 256 trois mille vers le seul Tyrol du nord; les Stubaier Alpen en possèdent 151. Citons à titre d'exemple Wildspitze (3.774 m) et Weisskugel (3.745 m) dans les Ötztaler Alpen, Zuckerhütl (3.507 m) et Schrankogel (3.495 m) dans les Stubaier Alpen. Les sommets situés entre Pitztal et Kaunertal présentent aux alpinistes un degré de difficulté élevé; de même les Kalkkögel — zone calcaire intercalée dans la roche primitive des Alpes Centrales — qui s'élèvent au-dessus de la Stubaital et des pistes olympiques de l'Axamer Lizum. Quelques avancées de ce système montagneux vers le sud ont pour ainsi dire formé des groupes indépendants: au sud-est les *Sarntaler Alpen*, région appropriée aux excursions et s'étendant entre Bolzano et Sterzing, Merano et Brixen; au sud-ouest, le groupe de la *Sesvenna*. Piz Sesvenna et Piz Lischana sont les dominantes du «Dreiländereck» entre le col de Reschen et celui d'Ofen. Sur cette région s'étend une grande partie du Parc National Suisse.

A l'est du Brenner (1.370 m), le col le plus important des Alpes Orientales où passe une voie ferrée et bientôt une autoroute, se dressent les sommets sauvages des *Zillertaler Alpen* (Hochfeiler, 3.523 m) et, moins élevées et très favorables à la pratique du ski, les *Tuxer Alpen*. Zillertal (Mayrhofen), Tuxertal et Gerlostal sont sillonées de téléphériques et remonte-pentes, de même d'ailleurs que les pentes du Patscherkofel et du Glungezer, deux montagnes familières aux skieurs. Dans ce domaine, Zillertaler et Tuxer Alpen sont encore largement dépassées par les *Kitzbühler Alpen*. Il s'agit en général de sommets schisteux aux pentes douces où foisonnent les différents mécanismes de remontée. Kitzbühel et Saalbach/Hinterglemm sont des stations très mondaines et de renommée mondiale. Les skieurs au portefeuille moins rempli trouveront d'aussi bonnes possibilités à Zell-am-See (Schmittenhöhe, Kirchberg, Hopfgarten, Alpbach et Wildschönau) ou dans d'autres petites localités de ce groupe divisé par la route passant au col de Thurn.

Faisant suite aux Zillertaler Alpen, nous trouvons le système très divisé des *Hohe Tauern*; plus long encore est le massif des *Niedere Tauern*. Dans les Hohe Tauern, nous sommes confrontés une fois encore avec des glaciers. Le Pasterze, glacier s'étendant entre le Grossglockner (3.798 m) — le plus haut sommet autrichien — et la Franz-Josef-Höhe, terminus de la «Gletscherstrasse», route qui bifurque de la route du Grossglockner, est même le plus important des Alpes Orientales. Il existe plusieurs possibilités de passer le massif des Hohe Tauern: la route du Glockner (altitude maxima 2.505 m) relie Bruck à Heiligenblut; la route du Felbertauern conduit de Mittersill au Tyrol Oriental et emprunte un tunnel long de 8,5 kilomètres percé en 1908. Les routes passant par les Radstädter Tauern — où a été aménagé Obertauern, nouveau centre de sports d'hiver — et par les Rottenmanner Tauern traversent les Niedere Tauern. Un grand dignitaire de l'Eglise, le prince-évêque de Gurk, Altgraf Salm-Reifferscheid, a décidé vers la fin du 18e siècle l'ascension du Grossglockner. On a d'abord aménagé des points d'appui; en 1799, on pouvait déjà planter une croix au sommet du Kleinglockner et, en 1800, on atteignait le sommet principal. En 1876, un margrave viennois, Alfred Pallavicini, avait atteint en compagnie de trois guides la brèche séparant le Kleinglockner du Grossglockner après avoir suivi le ravin qui porte son nom. Le guide Josef Tribusser a, paraît-il, taillé à lui seul 2500 marches dans la glace du ravin.

C'est en vain que l'archiduc Jean essaya en 1828 de faire l'ascension du Grossvenediger (3.674 m); il faudra attendre jusqu'en 1841 pour qu'une expédition dirigée par J. V. Kürsinger de Mittersill parvienne à atteindre cette calotte glaciaire visible depuis le haut-plateau bavarois. Une nouvelle technique de l'ascension sur la glace est née en 1924; cette année-là, le Dr. Willo Welzenbach, conseiller municipal munichois, utilisa pour la première fois des crampons pour l'ascension de la paroi nord-ouest du Grosses Wiesbachhorn. Au pied de cette paroi, dans la vallée de Kaprun, ont été aménagés d'immenses barrages (Moserboden, Limbergsperre) et un téléphérique permettant la pratique du ski en été sur le Grosses Kitzstein-

horn, à plus de 3.000 mètres d'altitude. Outre le groupe du *Glockner* et des *Venediger*, les Hohe Tauern comptent encore beaucoup de groupes importants tels que *Granatspitzgruppe* (Grosser Muntanitz, 3.231 m) et, plus à l'est *Goldberggruppe* (Hocharn, 3.251 m) et *Ankogel-Gruppe* (Hochalmspitze, 3.355 m); plus au sud, *Riesenfernergruppe* (Hochgall, 3.440 m), les *Villgratener Berge* qui forment la frontière entre le Tyrol Oriental et le Tyrol du Sud, *Schober-Gruppe* et *Kreuzeck-Gruppe*. Les Niedere Tauern culminent au Hochgolling (2.863 m). Les *Alpes Noriques* et les *Alpes Cétiques* constituent la limite orientale des Alpes Centrales.

*

Notre route nous conduit pour la dernière fois d'ouest en est, cette fois dans les *Alpes Orientales du Sud*. A l'est du massif de la Bernina, les Alpes de Livigno et de Bergame, nous rencontrons deux zones de glaciers et des sommets imposants. C'est le *massif de l'Ortler* qui s'étend entre Vintschgau et Sulzbergtal, puis le *groupe de l'Adamello* (3.554 m) et du Presanella (3.564 m). «König Ortler» (3.902 m) et Königsspitze (3.859 m) comptent parmi les principaux et les plus beaux sommets des Alpes Orientales. Ils s'élèvent au-dessus de Sulden et de Trafoi, citadelles de l'alpinisme et centres de sports d'hiver. Le Cevedale (3.769 m) offre lui aussi d'excellentes possibilités de pratiquer le ski. Comme pour beaucoup d'autres sommets, l'ascension de l'Ortler a été effectuée sur l'ordre d'une haute personnalité; l'archiduc Jean a exprimé ce désir et Josef Pichler, un chasseur de chamois, a trouvé le chemin du sommet le 27 septembre 1804. Les glaciers du massif de l'Ortler, le groupe de l'Adamello et la zone rocheuse difficilement praticable des Dolomites et des Alpes Carniques ont été de 1915 à 1918 le théâtre de violents combats dont les alpinistes découvrent les traces encore aujourd'hui. La route du Stilfserjoch a été construite dans des buts purement stratégiques. Ce col, le plus élevé des Alpes Orientales (2.757 m), est fermé en hiver; vers la fin du printemps et au début de l'été, par contre, les mécanismes de remontée fonctionnent sans arrêt.

Les *Nonsberger Alpen* sont orientées nord-sud; dans la Brenta, elles offrent d'excellentes conditions d'escalade et attirent ainsi nombre de touristes. Le centre principal en est Madonna di Campiglio; si la Cima Tosa (3.176 m) est le point culminant, le sommet le plus célèbre est par contre le Campanile Basso («Guglia di Brenta»). Les alpinistes considèrent souvent ce massif comme faisant partie des Dolomites car il manifeste une conformation géologique analogue. Mais Brenta et Dolomites sont séparées par la large vallée de l'Adige et par une zone montagneuse qui semble n'avoir pas encore été découverte par les touristes, les *Fleimstaler Alpen* (au-dessus de la vallée de l'Avisio). Les Dolomites proprement dites couvrent l'espace limité par l'Eggental au nord, la Pustertal et le col de Rolle au sud, l'Eisack à l'ouest et les *Belluneser Alpen* à l'est. Au sud de Trente, du massif de la Brenta et des Fleimstaler Alpen, la montagne s'abaisse nettement. C'est la région des *groupes de Brescia* et du *Lac de Garde*; du même genre sont, à l'est de l'Adige, les *Alpes de la région de Vicence*. Les *Dolomites* sont beaucoup trop différenciées pour qu'il soit possible de les évoquer en quelques lignes. Leur sommet principal est à la fois celui qui offre la plus grande variété: la Marmolata (3.344 m). Le versant nord est sillonné de mécanismes de remontée de toutes sortes et offre d'excellentes possibilités aux skieurs. Le versant sud, par contre, est réservé aux alpinistes éprouvés. «Il regno del sesto grado» (le royaume du sixième degré), tel est le nom que les Italiens donnent à la Civetta; pourtant, c'est la découverte des différentes routes permettant l'ascension de la paroi nord des Drei Zinnen qui a toujours fait sensation. L'ascension en 1925 de la paroi nord-ouest de la Civetta par deux Munichois, Solleder et Lettenbauer, et l'ascension de la paroi des Drei Zinnen par trois Italiens, Comici et les frères Dimai, en 1931 ont marqué le début d'une ère nouvelle de l'escalade. Au-dessus de Bolzano s'élève le Rosengarten avec ses différents sommets, les «Vajolettürme»; le Winklerturm, la plus audacieuse de ces tours, a été escaladée pour la première fois en 1887 par un lycéen munichois parti tout seul. Le centre principal des Dolomites est Cortina d'Ampezzo, ville olympique située au

pied du groupe de Tofana. Au-dessus du Val Gardena, théâtre des championnats du monde de ski en 1970, s'élèvent Langkofel et Stella. Au nord, les *monts de la région* de Sesto; au sud, dominant San Martino di Castrozza, la sauvage Pala. Ces quelques noms suffisent à peine à donner une idée de la merveilleuse beauté des Dolomites. Les nombreux cols (Gardena, Sella, Pardoijoch, Falzarego etc.) ont permis de construire quantité de routes — d'ailleurs excellentes — dont la présence a fait de cette montagne jadis impraticable une région touristique cherchant sa pareille dans l'ensemble de la chaîne des Alpes; c'est en outre un véritable paradis pour les skieurs.

Au-delà de la Piave, les *Alpes Carniques* s'étirent vers l'est. D'une étendue comparable à celle des Dolomites, ce massif est beaucoup moins connu, à part quelques exceptions; c'est par exemple le cas du Campanile di Val Montanaia, «la montagne la moins logique de toutes les Alpes», sommet très recherché des alpinistes. La crête principale du massif constitue la frontière austro-italienne. C'est là que se dressent les sommets les plus élevés (Hohe Warte, 2.787 m) et que se trouvent de nombreux refuges. Les routes traversent la partie sud du groupe d'est en ouest; elles passent par Sappada (où l'on parlait jadis allemand) et, plus au sud, par le col de Mauria.

Parallèles à la ligne des crêtes du groupe précédent, nous avons les *Gailtaler Alpen*, massif s'élevant entre les vallées de la Gail et de la Drave. Il va des «Dolomites de Lienz» jusqu'au Dobratsch, sommet célèbre pour son magnifique panorama.

Nous voici arrivés à l'extrémité des Alpes Orientales du Sud, dans une région où passent les frontières autrichienne, italienne et yougoslave. Trois groupes nous restent à mentionner: les *Karawanken* entre la Carinthie et la Slovénie (Hochstuhl, 2.239 m); les *Steiner Alpen*, massif de la région de Kamnik (Grintovec, 2.559 m), qui s'étendent presque entièrement sur le territoire yougoslave; les *Alpes Juliennes*. Du point de vue touristique, elles représentent la montagne yougoslave la plus importante. Notons toutefois qu'environ un tiers de ce massif appartient à l'Italie. La partie italienne (Wischberg, 2.666 m), et Montasch, 2.752 m) est une région assez solitaire; en Slovénie, par contre, on constate un enthousiasme énorme pour la plus haute montagne du pays. Cette région splendide a été adaptée au tourisme avec une perfection parfois même trop poussée. On a aménagé sur les parois difficiles plusieurs routes «audacieuses»; les nombreux refuges du Club Alpin de Slovénie (Planinska zveza Slovenije) offrent leur hospitalité à tous les alpinistes. Les trois nations en contact dans cette région vénèrent pareillement le Dr. Julius Kugy (1858 – 1944), Autrichien qui vivait à Trieste. C'est lui qui, en effet, a ouvert les Alpes Juliennes au tourisme. On lui a dédié un monument qui se dresse non loin du Triglav (2.863 m) point culminant des Alpes Juliennes des Slovénie. Les spécialistes de l'escalade qui viennent d'effectuer les 1.500 mètres de la paroi nord rencontrent au sommet les nombreux alpinistes partis de quatre refuges différents et qui ont emprunté des mon-tées préparées. Les vallées de la Save et de l'Isonzo (Soča) permettent de pénétrer facilement dans la montagne qui est traversée par des routes de cols intéressantes. Cette région montagneuse doit une partie de sa beauté à ses nombreux lacs: lac de Bohinj, lac de Bled et les sept lacs de la région du Triglav. Le haut-plateau de la Komna est un excellent centre de ski; c'est sur le tremplin de Planica que fut dépassée pour la première fois (1963) la limite des 100 mètres au saut à skis.

*

De Nice sur la Côte d'Azur à Ljubljana au sud du groupe s'élevant aux environs de Kamnik, nous avons parcouru environ 1.200 kilomètres. Quoique les impressions aient souvent varié, une formule n'en reste pas moins valable: «Pas de contrée plus belle …».

Index of Pictures — Index du photographies

© by Verlag Ludwig Simon, 8023 München-Pullach. – Verlags-Nr. 670. – Erich Pfeiffer-München besorgte die typographische Gestaltung. Beatrice Michaelis-Topping übernahm die englische und Jacqueline von Mengden die französische Übersetzung. Bei der Beschaffung der Aufnahmen waren u. a. der Bavaria-Verlag und die Bildagentur Kinkelin behilflich. – Gedruckt auf Phönix-Kunstdruckpapier der Papierfabrik Scheufelen. – Gesamtherstellung: R. Oldenbourg, Graphische Betriebe GmbH, München.

Printed in Germany – Imprimé en Allemagne

Der Montblanc (4807 m), höchster
Berg der Alpen und Europas,
Eisriese zwischen Frankreich und
Italien

Mont Blanc (15,782 ft), the highest
peak of the Alps and in Europe.
An ice-capped giant between
France and Italy

Le Mont Blanc (4807 m), point
culminant des Alpes et de l'Europe,
un géant de glace s'élevant entre la
France et l'Italie

Kapelle bei Les Tines im Tal von
Chamonix mit der Aiguille Verte
(4121 m) und den Aiguilles du Dru

Chapel near Les Tines in Chamonix
Valley with the peaks, Aiguille
Verte (13,520 ft) and the Aiguilles
du Dru

Chapelle près du village Les Tines
dans la vallée de Chamonix.
A l'arrière-plan, l'Aiguille Verte
(4121 m) et les Drus

42

Die Aiguille du Midi (3842 m), der „Aussichtsberg" für den Montblanc. 52 m unter dem Gipfel endet die Seilbahn

The Aiguille du Midi (12,605 ft), the place for the best view of Mont Blanc. The cable railway ends 170 ft below the peak

L'Aiguille du Midi (3842 m), sommet panoramique du Mont Blanc. Le terminus du téléphérique se trouve 52 mètres en dessous du sommet

Gletscherbruch im Vallée Blanche, dem gewaltigen Gletscher zwischen Aiguille du Midi und dem Mer de Glace

Glacial ice-fall in the Vallée Blanche, the vast glacier between Aiguille du Midi and Mer de Glace

Chaos glaciaire dans la Vallée Blanche, vaste glacier situé entre l'Aiguille du Midi et la Mer de Glace

Aiguille des Grands Charmoz
(3444 m) vom 1909 m hohen
Montenvers gesehen

The Aiguille des Grands Charmoz
(11,299 ft) viewed from
Montenvers at 6,263 ft

L'Aiguille des Grands Charmoz
(3444 m) vue de Montenvers,
à 1909 mètres d'altitude

45

Chamonix: Denkmal zur
Erinnerung an die Besteigung des
Montblanc durch H. B. de
Saussure mit Jacques Balmat

Monument in Chamonix erected to
commemorate the ascent of Mont
Blanc by H. B. de Saussure and
Jacques Balmat

Chamonix. Statue commémorant la
première ascension du Mont Blanc
par H. B. de Saussure et
Jacques Balmat

46

Blick von der Aiguille du Midi auf
Grandes Jorasses (4205 m),
Rochefortgrat und Dent du Géant

View from Aiguille du Midi
towards the Grandes Jorasses
(13,796 ft), Rochefort Ridge and
Dent du Géant

Les Grandes Jorasses (4205 m), la
Crête de Rochefort et la Dent du
Géant vues de l'Aiguille du Midi

47

Der Wintersport läßt ganze Orte neu entstehen, wie hier La Plagne in den Savoyer Alpen

Winter sports have given rise to entirely new resorts as here, La Plagne in the Savoy Alps

La Plagne, nouveau centre de sports d'hiver des Alpes de Savoie

Im Tal der Isère, umgeben von
hohen Bergen, liegt Grenoble,
die Hauptstadt der Dauphiné.
Internationaler Wintersportplatz
und Austragungsort der
Olympischen Winterspiele 1968

In the Isère Valley surrounded
by high mountains lies Grenoble,
the capital of the Dauphiné, an
international resort for winter sports
and where the Olympics of 1968
were staged

Grenoble, capitale du Dauphiné,
est blottie dans le Val d'Isère et
entourée de sommets majestueux.
Centre de sports d'hiver de renommée
mondiale, Grenoble a organisé
les Jeux Olympiques d'hiver 1968

49

Blick vom Col de la Croix-de-Fer
(2078 m) auf das Massiv der
Belledonne-Kette

View from the Col
de la Croix de Fer (6,818 ft)
towards the Belladonna Chain

Le Massif de Belledonne vu du col
de la Croix-de-Fer (2078 m)

In malerischer Lage, am felsigen
Hang über der Vernaison,
das Städtchen Pont-en-Royans

The little town of Pont en Royans,
picturesquely situated on the rocky
slope above the Vernaison

Pont-en-Royans, petite localité
pittoresque suspendue au rocher,
domine la Vernaison

51

Auf eine Höhe von 1600 m steigt
diese kühne Serpentinenstraße nach
Montevernier hinauf. Tiefblick in
das Arctal bei St-Jean-de-
Maurienne

The bold curves of the serpentine
road to Montevernier which rises to
an altitude of 5280 ft. A view down
into the Arc Valley near St. Jean de
Maurienne

Téméraire, cette route en lacet
s'élève sur une hauteur de 1600
mètres jusqu'à Montevernier. Vue
sur la vallée de l'Arc aux environs
de St-Jean-de-Maurienne

Drac-Tal südlich von Grenoble an
der Route Napoleon mit Blick
zum Pelvoux-Massiv (Dauphiné-
Alpen)

Drac Valley south of Grenoble on
the Route Napoleon, with a view
towards the Pelvoux Massif
(Dauphiné Alps)

La vallée du Drac au sud de
Grenoble, vue de la Route
Napoléon. A l'arrière-plan, le
massif du Pelvoux dans les Alpes
du Dauphiné

53

In den Cottischen Alpen, am Monte Viso, in 1952 m Höhe, entspringt der größte Fluß Italiens, der 672 km lange Po

At an altitude of 6432 ft, in the Cottian Alps, Italy's longest river, the Po rises. It is 420 mls long

Le Pô (672 km), le principal fleuve d'Italie, prend sa source dans les Alpes à 1952 m d'altitude

Sestrière, 2035 m auf dem Sattel zwischen dem Chisone-Tal und dem Tal der Dora Riparia, einer der bedeutendsten Wintersportplätze Europas

Sestrière, on the saddle between the Chisone-Valley and that of Dora Riparia, is one of Europe's most important winter-sports centres (6,677 ft)

Située sur une hauteur séparant les vallées du Chisone et de la Doire Ripaire, Sestrière 2035 m compte parmi les principales stations de sports d'hiver européennes

Die dreigipfelige Meije in den Dauphiné-Alpen, einer der wildesten und erhabensten Berge der Alpen

The three peaks of the Meije in the Dauphiné Alps form one of the wildest and grandest Alpine mountains

Avec ses trois sommets, la Meije (Alpes du Dauphiné) offre un aspect sauvage et digne à la fois

56

Im oberen Guital, durch das vermutlich Hannibal mit seinen Elefanten zog, das alte Bergdorf St. Véran

The ancient mountain village of St. Véran lies in the Upper Gui Valley, through which Hannibal and his elephants presumably passed

St-Véran, vieux village de montagne de la haute-vallée du Gui. Hannibal a vraisemblablement emprunté cette vallée lors de sa traversée des Alpes avec ses éléphants

57

Im Grand Cañon du Verdon, der bis zu 700 m tiefen, gewaltigsten und eindrucksvollsten Schlucht Europas

In the Grand Cañon of Verdon, the most stupendous and impressive gorge in Europe with a maximum depth of 2297 ft

La gorge du Verdon atteint jusqu'à 700 mètres de profondeur, c'est la plus importante et la plus imposante d'Europe

Das alte Sisteron, an der Mündung des Buech in die Durance, eng an senkrecht aufsteigenden Kalkwänden gelegen

Ancient Sisteron, where the Buech flows into the Durance, clings to the sheer limestone mountain faces

Au confluent du Buech et de la Durance, ces maisons de Sisteron semblent collées à la paroi calcaire presque verticale

60 Über dem Valnontey erhebt sich der
mächtige Gran Paradiso (4061 m)

Rising above the Valnontey, the
mighty Gran Paradiso (13,323 ft)

Le Gran Paradiso (4061 m) domine
le Valnontey

Durch das Tal des Artanavaz führt
die Straße zum Großen St. Bernhard (2469 m)

The road to the Great St. Bernhard
(8,100 ft) Pass leads through the
Artanavaz Valley

La route conduisant au Grand
St-Bernard (2469 m) traverse la
vallée de l'Artanavaz

61

Blick über die Rochers de Naye
(2042 m)

Aerial view of Rochers de Naye

Vue sur les Rochers de Naye
(2042 m)

Schloß Chillon am Genfer See,
eine alte Burg der Herzöge von
Savoyen, mit den Dents du Midi
(3257 m)

Chillon Castle on the Lake of
Geneva is the ancestral home of
the Dukes of Savoy. The mountain
is Dents du Midi (10,686 ft)

Le château de Chillon, l'antique
manoir des ducs de Savoie, fut
construit dès le IXᵉ siècle ▶

Der Mount Ruan in der Nähe von Champéry

Mont Ruan near Champéry

Le Mont Ruan, aux environs de Champéry

Der Kirchturm von Champéry und
die Dents du Midi (3257 m)

The spire of Champéry and Dents
du Midi (10,686 ft)

Le clocher de Champéry et les
Dents du Midi (3257 m)

65

Die unvergleichliche Felspyramide
des Matterhorns (4478 m), des
„Berges aller Berge", bei Zermatt

The peerless rock pyramid of the
Matterhorn (14,705 ft), the "acme
of all mountains" near Zermatt

La gigantesque pyramide du
Matterhorn (4478 m), la «montagne
des montagnes», près de Zermatt

Monte Rosa: Die Dufourspitze, mit 4634 m höchster Gipfel der Schweiz

Monte Rosa: Dufour Peak (15,217 ft) is the highest summit in Switzerland

Monte Rosa: La Pointe Dufour (4634 m), le plus haut sommet de Suisse

Die gewaltigen Eisströme des
Theodul- und des Gorner-Gletschers

These gigantic streams of ice are the
Theodul and the Gorner Glaciers

Les imposants fleuves de glace des
glaciers de Theodul et du Gorner

Das Zinalrothorn (4223 m) und der Moming-Gletscher

The Zinalrothorn (13,855 ft) and the Moming Glacier

Le Zinalrothorn (4223 m) et le glacier du Moming

Riesen der Walliser Alpen: Das
Weißhorn (4506 m), im Hintergrund
das Matterhorn (4478 m) und
rechts Dent d'Hérens (4171 m)

Giants of the Pennine Alps:
Weisshorn (14,783 ft), in the background, the Matterhorn (14,705 ft)
and right, the Dent d'Herens

Un géant des Alpes Valaisannes:
le Weisshorn (4506 m). A l'arrière-
plan, le Matterhorn (4478 m); à
droite, la Dent d'Hérens (4171 m)

Das Kirchlein in Ried unter den
Gletschern ist charakteristisch für
das Wallis

The little chapel at Ried under the
glaciers is typical of Valais

Cette chapelle de Ried, village
situé au pied des glaciers, est
typique du Valais

Straße nach St. Luc im Val
d'Anniviers/Wallis

The road to St. Luc in the
Anniviers Valley (Valais)

Cette route conduit à St-Luc dans
le Val d'Anniviers (Valais)

Das Obergabelhorn (4063 m) über der Cabane du Mountet (2886 m) des S.A.C.

The Obergabelhorn (13,330 ft) above the S.A.C.'s Cabane du Mountet (9469 ft)

L'Obergabelhorn (4063 m) au-dessus de la Cabane du Mountet (2886 m), refuge du Club Alpin Suisse

73

Kandersteg, überragt von Wildstrubel, Tschingellochtighorn und
Großem und Kleinem Lohner

Wildstrubel, Tschingellochtighorn
and Großer and Kleiner Lohner
tower above Kandersteg

Kandersteg d'où l'on voit le Wildstrubel, le Tschingellochtighorn,
le Grand et le Petit Lohner

◀ Der Oeschinensee (1578 m)
unterhalb der Blümlisalpgruppe
(3664 m), ein Glanzpunkt der
Berner Alpen

Oeschinensee (5177 ft) below the
Blümlisalp Group (12,021 ft) a
highlight in the Bernese Alps

L'Oeschinensee, lac situé à 1578
mètres, est dominé par la
Blümlisalp (3664 m), l'un des plus
jolis sommets des Alpes Bernoises

75

76   Blick auf Gstaad mit Wildhorn,   Gstaad with Wildhorn, Gelten   Gstaad avec son palace. A l'arrière-plan le
        Geltengletscher und Windspielen   Glacier and Windspielen   Wildhorn, le glacier Gelten et le Windspielen

Standseilbahn Mürren—Allmendhubel, im Hintergrund das
Lauterbrunner Breithorn (3782 m)

Mürren—Allmendhubel Funicular
Railway, with Breithorn (12,408 ft)
in the background

Le chemin de fer à crémaillère
Mürren—Allmendhubel; à l'arrière-
plan le Breithorn (3782 m)

Motiv im „Gletscherdorf" Grindelwald

In the "glacier-village" of Grindelwald

Grindelwald, motif du «village-glacier»

Durch eine grandiose Landschaft führt
die Jungfraubahn zum höchsten Bahnhof
Europas in 3454 m Höhe. —
Jungfrau, Schneehorn und Silberhorn

The Jungfrau Railway passes through
magnificent scenery on the way to the
highest station in Europe at 11,332 ft.
Jungfrau, Schneehorn and Silberhorn

Le funiculaire «Jungfraubahn» traverse
un paysage grandiose avant d'atteindre
le terminus à 3454 mètres.
Jungfrau, Schneehorn et Silberhorn

78

Hier ist die ganze Majestät des Berner Oberlandes eingefangen: das Tal von Lauterbrunnen mit dem gewaltigen Talschluß; vorn auf der Terrasse Wengen, unten im Talgrund Lauterbrunnen, rechts der Staubbachfall; im Hintergrund Mittaghorn, Breithorn, Tschingelhorn, Tschingelspitz und Gspaltenhorn

An incomparable picture! The Valley of Lauterbrunnen with the magnificent barrier at its head; in front, Wengen on the terrace; below, Lauterbrunnen, to the right, Staubbach Fall; in the background, Mittaghorn, Breithorn, Tschingelhorn, Tschingelspitz and Gspaltenhorn

L'Oberland bernois dans toute sa splendeur: la vallée de Lauterbrunnen; sur la terrasse au premier plan, le village de Wengen; plus bas, le village de Lauterbrunnen; à droite, la cascade du Staubbach. A l'arrière-plan, le Mittaghorn, le Breithorn, le Tschingelhorn, le Pic du Tschingel et le Gspaltenhorn

82 Im Männlichengebiet mit Mönch, Tschuggen und Jungfrau

In the Männlichen District. Mönch Tschuggen and Jungfrau

Dans la plaine du Männlichen. Au fond le Mönch, Tschuggen et la Jungfrau

Station Birg der Schilt-
horn-Bahn mit Mönch
und Jungfrau

Birg Station on the
Schilthorn Railway with
Mönch and Jungfrau
in view

La station Birg du
téléphérique du Schilt-
horn avec le Mönch et
la Jungfrau

Der Gletscherzirkus des
Blümlisalphorns (3664 m)

The "Glacier Circus" on the
Blümlisalphorn (12,021 ft)

Le cirque glaciaire de la
Blümlisalp (3664 m)

Die Kleine Scheidegg (2064 m) am Fuß der gewaltigen Eiger-Nordwand (3974 m)

Kleine Scheidegg (6772 ft) at the foot of the mighty Eiger North Wall (13,042 ft)

La petite Scheidegg (2064 m) au pied de l'imposante paroi nord de l'Eiger (3974 m)

85

Blick von der Sustenpaßstraße
über den Steingletscher (links) zum
3435 m hohen Gwächtenhorn

View from the Susten Pass Road
across the Stein Glacier (left) to
the Gwächtenhorn (11,270 ft)

Le Steingletscher (à gauche) et le
Gwächtenhorn (3435 m) vus de la
route du col de Susten

Bergsteiger am Gipfel der Fünffingerstöcke in den Berner Alpen

Mountain climbers on the summit of the Fünffingerstöcke in the Bernese Alps

Alpinistes au sommet des Fünffingerstöcke dans les Alpes Bernoises

87

Der Obergletscher bei Grindelwald, zwischen dem Wetterhorn (3701 m) und dem über 4000 m hohen Schreckhorn

The Upper Glacier near Grindelwald, between Wetterhorn (12,149 ft) and Schreckhorn (almost 13,750 ft)

L'Obergletscher près de Grindelwald, entre le Wetterhorn (3701 m) et le Schreckhorn (plus de 4000 m)

Der Weltkurort Interlaken mit
Mönch und Jungfrau (4158 m)

Interlaken, an international resort
with the Mönch and Jungfrau Peaks

Interlaken, station de villégiature des
plus réputées de Suisse, est dominée
par le Mönch et la Jungfrau

89

90   Blick von Brünig-Hasliberg auf
Wetterhorn, Mönch und Eiger

View from Brünig-Hasliberg towards
Wetterhorn, Mönch and Eiger

Vue du Brünig-Hasliberg sur le
Wetterhorn, le Mönch et l'Eiger

Andermatt, ein bekannter Wintersportplatz im Herzen der Zentralschweiz

Andermatt, a well-known wintersports
resort, lies in the heart of central Switzerland

Andermatt, célèbre station de
sports d'hiver en Suisse Centrale

Im Skigebiet von Trübsee oberhalb
Engelberg

The skiing slopes of Trübsee above
Engelberg

Trübsee, véritable eldorado des
skieurs, est situé au-dessus d'Engelberg

Ausblick vom Großen Spannort
(3199 m) auf die Berge der
Zentralschweiz

Panorama seen from the Grosse
Spannort (10,496 ft) in the central
Swiss Alps

Les sommets de la Suisse Centrale
vus du Grand Spannort (3199 m)

94   Blick vom Pilatus über Bürgenstock   View from Pilatus over the   Du Pilate, le regard embrasse le Bürgen-
      und Vierwaldstätter See   Bürgenstock and Lake Lucerne   stock et le Lac des Quatre-Cantons

Föhnsturm über dem Urner See

Southerly storm (Foehn) over Lake Urn

Sur l'Urner See, quand le Foehn souffle en tempête

95

Die Kantonshauptstadt Glarus mit
dem Vorder-Glärnisch (2331 m)

The cantonal capital of Glarus
with Vorder-Glärnisch (7648 ft)

Glarus, chef-lieu de canton, et le
Vorder-Glärnisch (2331 m)

In unzähligen Windungen schlängelt
sich die Straße vom Maloja-Paß
(1817 m) hinab ins Bergell

In countless hair-pin bends the
road snakes up to Maloja Pass at
over 5961 ft

Cette route en lacet descend du col
de la Maloja (1817 m) vers le Val
Bregaglia

97

98   Soglio im Bergell, malerisch auf einer Hangterrasse oberhalb des Meratales gelegen   Soglio in Bergell, lies picturesquely on a sloping terrace above the Mera Valley   Soglio dans le Val Bregaglia s'est installée de manière pittoresque sur une terrasse naturelle dominant la vallée de la Mera

Blick vom Morteratsch-Gletscher
auf den Piz Bernina (4049 m)

View of Piz Bernina (13,304 ft)
from the Morteratsch Glacier

Le Piz Bernina vu du glacier
de Morteratsch

Der berühmte Biancograt zum Piz
Bernina (4049 m)

The renowned Bianco Ridge on
the Bernina (13,304 ft)

Sur la célèbre arête de Bianco,
lors de l'ascension vers le Piz
Bernina (4049 m)

„Das Silberschloß": Piz Palü-
Ostgipfel in der Bernina-Gruppe

The "Silver Castle" of Piz Palu,
the eastern peak in the Bernina
Group

Le Piz Palü encore appelé
«Silberschloss» (château d'argent)
dans l'est du massif de la Bernina

101

Aufstieg zur Crast Agüzza   The climb up to Crast Agüzza   Pendant la montée vers la Crast Agüzza

Schloß Tarasp im Engadin gegen
Piz Lischana (3109 m)

Tarasp Castle in the Engadine;
view towards Piz Lischana
(10,200 ft)

Le château de Tarasp dans
l'Engadine avec le Piz Lischana
(3109 m) à l'arrière-plan

Der Kleine Piz Buin mit dem
Piz Linard (3414 m, links im
Hintergrund), dem höchsten Gipfel
der Silvretta-Gruppe, vom Aufstieg
104   zum Großen Piz Buin (3316 m)

The Little Piz Buin with Piz Linard
(11,168 ft), in the left background,
the highest peak in the Silvretta
Group; view from the way up to
the Great Piz Buin (10,879 ft)

Le Petit Piz Buin; à gauche, à
l'arrière-plan, le Piz Linard (3414 m),
point culminant du massif de la
Silvretta. Vue prise pendant la montée vers le Grand Piz Buin (3316 m)

Die Dreiländerspitze (3225 m) in
der Silvretta, auf der Grenze
zwischen Vorarlberg, Tirol und
Graubünden gelegen

The Dreiländer Spitze (10,581 ft)
in the Silvrettas, at the juncture of
the frontiers of Vorarlberg, Tyrol
and Grisons

La Dreiländerspitze (3225 m),
sommet du massif de la Silvretta,
s'élève entre Vorarlberg, Tyrol et
Grisons

Der 3902 m hohe „König Ortler"　　　　"King Ortler", 12,799 ft　　　　Le «Roi Ortler», sommet majestueux
atteignant 3902 mètres

Die 1820—24 erbaute und seitdem in der Trassierung unveränderte Stilfser-Joch-Straße erreicht in 48 Kehren 2756 m Höhe

The Stilfser Joch Road, constructed in 1820—24 and since then unaltered in its lay-out, requires 48 bends to reach a height of 9042 ft

Aménagée entre 1820 et 1824, la route du Stilfser-Joch a conservé son tracé primitif; ses 48 virages conduisent jusqu'à 2756 mètres d'altitude

Tschagguns im Montafon,
im Hintergrund die Drei Türme
(2755 m) und die Drusenfluh

Tschagguns in Montafon;
in the background, the Drei Türme
(9039 ft) and the Drusenfluh

Tschagguns dans le Montafon;
à l'arrière-plan, «Drei Türme»
(2755 m) et Drusenfluh

Blick von der Ulmer Hütte
(2285 m) über den Arlbergpaß
und St. Christoph ins Ferwall

View from the Ulm Hut (7496 ft)
above the Arlberg Pass and
St. Christoph into the Fervall

De la «Ulmer Hütte», refuge situé à 2285 mètres,
on jouit d'une vue magnifique sur le col de l'Arlberg
et St-Christophe; au loin, la zone du Ferwall

Stuben am Arlberg, Wintersportplatz und Geburtsort des
Skipioniers Hannes Schneider

Stuben on the Arlberg, winter-
sports resort and birth-place of the
skiing pioneer, Hannes Schneider

Stuben sur l'Arlberg, station de sports
d'hiver et lieu de naissance de Hannes
Schneider, pionnier du ski

Die Antoniuskapelle im Wilden
Kaiser gegen Totenkirchl,
Karlspitzen, Kleine Halt, Ellmauer
Halt und Sonneck

St. Antony's Chapel in the Wilder
Kaiser towards Totenkirchl,
Karlspitzen, Kleine Halt, Ellmauer
Halt and Sonneck

La chapelle St-Antoine dans le
Wilder Kaiser; à l'arrière-plan,
Totenkirchl, Karlspitzen, Petite
Halt, Ellmauer Halt et Sonneck

112 In der grandiosen Bergwelt der
Zillertaler Alpen

The magnificence of the high alps in
the Zillertal Mountains is overwhelming

Majesté imposante des montagnes
de la Zillertal

Der Große Mörchner (3283 m) und
die Mörchenschneidspitze (3230 m)
über der Floite

Rising above the Floite, the Great
Mörchner (10,771 ft) and the
Mörchenschneid Spitze (10,597 ft)

Le Grand Mörchner (3283 m) et la
Mörchenschneidespitze (3230 m)
dominent la Floite

113

◀ Innsbruck, alte Tiroler
Landeshauptstadt. Maria-
Theresien-Straße mit der
1706 errichteten Anna-
säule und der Nordkette
im Hintergrund

Innsbruck, the old capital
of Tyrol. Maria Theresia
Str. with the St. Anna
Column (1706) and the
Nordkette in the back-
ground

Innsbruck, capitale du
Tyrol. La Rue Marie-
Thérèse avec la colonne
Ste-Anne (1706); à
l'arrière-plan, la Nordkette

▶

Stubaier Alpen. Der
Schrankogel (3496 m) aus
dem Aufstieg von der
Amberger Hütte (2135 m)
zur Hochstubaihütte
(3173 m)

In the Stubai Alps,
Schrankogel (11,470 ft)
seen from the climbers'
path from the Amberg
Hut (6677 ft) to the Hoch
Stubai Hut (10,410 ft)

Stubaier Alpen.
Le Schrankogel (3496 m)
tel qu'il apparaît lors de
l'ascension de l'Amberger
Hütte (refuge situé à
2135 m) vers la Hoch-
stubaihütte (autre refuge
à 3173 m)

Ötztaler Alpen: Blick von der
Hohen Geige (3395 m) zur
Watzespitze (3533 m) im
Kaunergrat

Ötztal Alps: view from the Hohe
Geige (11,139 ft) to the Watze
Spitze (11,591 ft) in the Kauner
Ridge

Ötztaler Alpen. La Wartespitze
(3533 m) dans le Kaunergrat vue
de la Hohe Geige (3395 m)

Ötztaler Alpen: Im Skigebiet von
Hochsölden. Die Innere Schwarze
Schneide (3369 m) gesehen von
der Rotkogelhütte (2662 m)

Ötztal Alps: the Hochsölden
skiing grounds. The Innere
Schwarze Schneide (11,053 ft) seen
from the Rotkogel Hut (8734 ft)

Ötztaler Alpen. Au centre de ski
de Hochsölden. Innere Schwarze
Schneide (3369 m) vue du refuge
Rotkogelhütte (2662 m)

117

Hoher First (3405 m) und
Granatenkogel (3304 m) im
118   Hauptkamm der Ötztaler Alpen

Hoher First (11,171 ft) and
Granatenkogel (10,840 ft) in the
Main Ridge of the Ötztal Alps

Hoher First (3405 m) et
Granatenkogel (3304 m) dans l'arête
principale des Ötztaler Alpen

Stillachtal bei Einödsbach
mit Trettachspitze und
Mädelegabel (2645 m)

Stillach Valley near Einödsbach
with Trettach Spitze
and Mädelegabel (8678 ft)

Près de Einödsbach, la vallée de la Stillach
est surplombée par la Trettachspitze
et la Mädelegabel (2645 m)

119

Der Seekogel (3358 m) überragt den
Riffelsee über dem Pitztal

Seekogel (11,017 ft) towers above
Riffelsee, a lake lying high above
the Pitz Valley

Le Seekogel (3358 m) domine le
Riffelsee et la Pitztal

Zirl, ein freundlicher Ort im Inntal, mit der Ruine Fragenstein. Im Hintergrund die Kalkkögel

The ruins of Fragenstein dominate Zirl, a friendly place in the Inn Valley. Kalkkögel in the background

Zirl, gentille localité de la vallée de l'Inn, est dominée par les ruines de Fragenstein. A l'arrière-plan, les Kalkkögel

121

In den Tannheimer Bergen:
Kellespitze (2247 m) und Gimpel
(2176 m) über der Musauer Alp
im Reintal

In the Tannheim Alps; Kelle
Spitze (7372 ft) and Gimpel
(7139 ft) rise above Musau Alp in
the Rein Valley

Dans le massif des Tannheimer.
Kellespitze (2247 m) et Gimpel
(2176 m) surplombent la Musauer
Alp, chalet de la vallé de Rein

Schloß Neuschwanstein über dem
Alpsee, das Märchenschloß des
Königs Ludwig II. Touristen-
attraktion Nummer 1 in Oberbayern

Neuschwanstein Castle above
Alpsee; the fairy-tale castle of
King Ludwig II, is Upper
Bavaria's tourist attraction No. 1

Le château de Neuschwanstein et
l'Alpsee; ce château féerique du roi
Louis II est l'attraction touristique
numéro un de la Haute-Bavière

123

Das wilde Bacherloch über Einödsbach; am Horizont der 1962 umgefallene Felsturm des Wilden Männle

The wild Bacherloch above Einödsbach; on the sky-line, the "Rocky Tower" of the Wildes Männle, which overturned in 1962

Site sauvage du Bacherloch audessus de l'Einödsbach. A l'horizon, la tour rocheuse du Wildes Männle qui s'est écroulée en 1962

Ammergauer Alpen: Blick vom
Pürschling in das Graswangtal bei
Oberammergau

Ammergau Alps: view from
Pürschling into Graswang Valley
near Oberammergau

Dans les monts de l'Ammergau.
La vallée de Graswang près
d'Oberammergau vue du Pürschling   125

Die Dreitorspitze (2682 m) im
Wettersteingebirge vom Kreuzeck

Dreitor Spitze (8819 ft) in the
Wetterstein Range, seen from
Kreuzeck

La Dreitorspitze (2682 m) dans
le massif du Wetterstein vue du
Kreuzeck

Blick vom „Ehrwalder Becken"
(Lermoos) auf das Wettersteingebirge mit Zugspitze

View from the "Ehrwald Basin"
(Lermoos), the view towards the
Wetterstein Range with Zug Spitze

Le massif du Wetterstein et la
Zugspitze vus de l'«Ehrwalder
Becken» (Lermoos)

◀ Die Alpspitze: eine der
markantesten Gestalten
der deutschen Alpenwelt!
Wuchtig und doch wohl-
geformt wächst sie aus
dem Werdenfelser Land
empor, 2620 m hoch

Alp Spitze: one of the
most striking formations
of the German alpine
region! Massive and yet
well-shaped, it soars up
from the Werdenfels
Land to 8616 ft

L'Alpspitze (2620 m),
un des sommets les plus
caractéristiques des Alpes
de Bavière. Massive et
pourtant élégante, elle
s'élève au-dessus du
Werdenfelser Land

Am Rande des Murnauer ▶
Mooses liegt Eschenlohe
mit seiner reizvollen
Pfarrkirche. Im Hinter-
grund die Hohe Kiste
(1922 m)

Eschenlohe, with a charm-
ing Parish Church, lies
on the edge of the Murnau
Moos. In the background,
Hohe Kiste (6306 ft)

A la lisière du Murnauer
Moos, Eschenlohe avec
sa charmante église
paroissiale. A l'arrière-
plan, la Hohe Kiste
(1922 m)

Geroldsee bei Mittenwald
mit Karwendel: Tiefkar-
spitze (2431 m), Larchet-
fleckspitze (2250 m),
Westliche Karwendel-
spitze (2385 m)

Geroldsee near Mitten-
wald with Karwendel,
Tiefkar Spitze (7976 ft),
Larchetfleck Spitze
(7379 ft) and the West
Karwendel Spitze (7824 ft)

Le Geroldsee, lac des
environs de Mittenwald.
A l'arrière-plan, se mirant
dans le lac, les sommets
du Karwendel: Tiefkar-
spitze (2431 m), Larchet-
fleckspitze (2250 m),
Karwendelspitze (2385 m)

Mittenwald, der bekannte
Ferienort am Fuße des
Karwendelgebirges

Mittenwald, the well-
known holiday place at
the foot of the Karwendel
Range

Mittenwald, célèbre lieu
de villégiature au pied du
Karwendel

131

Die Spritzkarspitze (2609 m) im Karwendel, vom Großen Ahornboden aus gesehen

Spritzkar Spitze (8580 ft), in the Karwendel Range, seen from the Great Ahornboden

La Spritzkarspitze (2609 m), sommet du Karwendel, vue du Grand Ahornboden

132

Morgenstimmung auf dem
Herzogstand (1731 m). Blick über
den Walchensee zum Guffert

Dawn on the Herzogstand
(5679 ft). View across Lake
Walchen towards Guffert

Impression matinale sur le
Herzogstand (1731 m). Vue sur
le Walchensee et le Guffert

Bekannte Ferienziele in Oberbayern: Schliersee und (rechts)
Rottach-Egern am Tegernsee. —
Hier lebten Ludwig Thoma und
134 Ludwig Ganghofer

Well-known holiday centres in
Upper Bavaria: Schliersee and
(right) Rottach-Egern on Tegernsee
Lake, where Ludwig Thoma and
Ludwig Ganghofer lived

Lieux de séjour très cotés:
Schliersee et, à droite, Rottach-
Egern au bord du Tegernsee. —
Ludwig Thoma et Ludwig
Ganghofer ont vécu là

Chiemgauer Alpen. Blick von der Scharte unter dem Geigelstein (1808 m) zum Wilden Kaiser

Chiemgau Alps: the view from the "Scharte" (Gap) under the Geigelstein (5932 ft) towards the Wilder Kaiser

Dans les Alpes du Chiemgau. Le Wilder Kaiser (1808 m) vu du Geigelstein

Neubeuern, ein idyllischer Flecken
im Inntal

Neubeuern, a picturesque place in
the Inn Valley

Neubeuern, site idyllique de la
vallée de l'Inn

Anger, das „schönste
Dorf Bayerns", wie es
einst König Ludwig II.
nannte, gegen Hoch-
staufen und Zwiesel

Anger, the "loveliest
village in Bavaria" as
King Ludwig II once
called it, looking towards
Hochstaufen and Zwiesel

Anger qui, selon Louis II,
est le plus joli village de
Bavière. A l'arrière-plan,
Hochstaufen et Zwiesel

Unter dem Gipfelkreuz
des Hochstaufens (1771 m)
bei Bad Reichenhall

Under the cross on the summit
of Hochstaufen (5810 ft) near
Bad Reichenhall

Halte au sommet du
Hochstaufen (1771 m)
près de Bad Reichenhall

139

Typisches ,,Oberbayern"
und nicht nur ,,Touristen-
Gaudi" bietet sich in Reit
im Winkl und in Inzell
(unten)

Scenes typical of Upper
Bavaria and not only
shows put on for the
tourists are to be seen at
Reit im Winkl and at
Inzell (below)

Reit-im-Winkl et Inzell
(en bas) offrent des images
typiques de Haute Bavière
et non un amusement
pour les touristes

Mit der Seilbahn auf den
1636 m hohen Rauschberg
bei Ruhpolding

Going up the Rauschberg
(5368 ft) near Ruhpolding,
by cable car

Ce téléphérique conduit
sur le Rauschberg
(1636 m), sommet des
environs de Ruhpolding

Ein besonders eigenartiges
Felsgebilde: Steinerne Agnes im
Lattengebirge

A unique rock formation in the
Latten Mountains, called the
"Stone Agnes"

Un rocher aux formes bien
bizarres: «Steinerne Agnès» dans
le Lattengebirge

Blick von der Deutschen
Alpenstraße bei Ramsau auf die
Reiteralpe

View from the German Alpine
Road near Ramsau towards
Reiteralpe

La Reiteralpe vue de la «Route des
Alpes» près de Ramsau

Die Hochkalter-Gruppe in den Berchtesgadener Alpen birgt den einzigen Gletscher Deutschlands, das Blaueis

The Hochkalter Group in the Berchtesgaden Alps contains the only German glacier, the "Blue Ice"

Le Blaueis, le seul glacier d'Allemagne, se trouve dans les Hochkalter, groupe du massif de Berchtesgaden

St. Bartholomä am Königssee und
die berühmte Watzmann-Ostwand,
bei einer Höhe von 1800 m die
höchste Wand der Ostalpen

St. Bartholomä on Königssee, and
the notorious Watzmann East
Wall; with a rise of 5906 ft,
it is the sheerest rock face in the
Eastern Alps

St-Bartholomé au bord du
Königssee et le célèbre versant est
du Watzmann; haute de 1800
mètres, cette paroi rocheuse est la
plus importante des Alpes Orientales

◀ Berchtesgaden und
Watzmann (2713 m)

Berchtesgaden and the
Watzmann (8901 ft)

Berchtesgaden et le
Watzmann (2713 m)

▶

Die wildzerrissene
Manndlwand im Hoch-
könig-Massiv der
Berchtesgadener Alpen
umfaßt 37 benannte
Felstürme

The craggy Manndl Face
in the Hochkönig Massif
of the Berchtesgaden Alps
contains 37 named crags

Le «Manndlwand»,
montagne déchiquetée
du groupe du Hochkönig
(massif de Berchtesgaden)
compte 37 tours rocheuses

Blick von der Madlschneid auf
Weißenbach am Attersee und den
Schafberg

Looking down from Madlschneid
towards Weissenbach on Lake
Attersee, and Schafberg

Weissenbach sur l'Attersee et le
Schafberg vus du haut du
Madlschneid

Hallstatt, benannt nach dem schon in frühgeschichtlicher Zeit betriebenen Salzbergbau

Hallstatt, famous for its salt mines which were worked in the earliest historical times

Hallstatt est célèbre pour ses mines de sel gemme exploitées depuis des temps très lointains

149

Klettern im Fels: Abseilen am Steinberg in der Hochkaltergruppe und an den ,,Führernadeln'' im Wilden Kaiser (links)

Rock-climbing: roping down the Steinberg in the Hochkalter Group and on the ''Fuhrernadeln'' in the Wilder Kaiser Mountains

Haute école de varappe: descente en rappel au Steinberg (groupe des Hochkalter) et, à gauche, aux «Führernadeln» dans le massif du Wilder Kaiser

Das Skiparadies der Tauplitzalm
mit dem Lawinenstein (1984 m)
im Toten Gebirge/Steiermark

A paradise for skiers on the Tauplitz
Alm, with the Lawinenstein (6509 ft)
in the Toten Gebirge in Styria

Eldorado des skieurs à la Tauplitzalm
dans le Totes Gebirge (Styrie);
à l'arrière-plan, le Lawinenstein (1984 m)

Stausee Mooserboden im
Kapruner Tal
(Glockner Gruppe)

Mooserboden Reservoir in the
Kaprun Valley
(Glockner Group)

Le lac de barrage de Mooserboden
dans la vallée de Kaprun (groupe
des Glockner)

Blick zur Großen Bischofsmütze (2455 m) im Gosaukamm der Dachsteingruppe

A view towards Great Bischofsmütze (8055 ft) in the Gosau Ridge of the Dachstein Group

La Grande Bischofsmütze (2455 m) dans le groupe du Dachstein

Venediger-Gruppe. Der Große
Geiger (3365 m) von der
Kürsingerhütte (2553 m)

From the Kürsing Hut (8376 ft)
in the Venediger Group, a view
of the Great Geiger (11,040 ft)

Dans les Venediger. Le Grand
Geiger (3365 m) vu de la Kürsingerhütte,
refuge situé à 2553 mètres d'altitude

Der Großglockner (3798 m)
überragt die Pfarrkirche und
den Bergsteigerfriedhof von
156   Heiligenblut (1301 m)

Gross Glockner (12,461 ft) towers
above the Parish Church and the
mountaineers' graveyard at
Heiligenblut (4268 ft)

Le Grossglockner (3798 m)
domine l'église de Heiligenblut
(1301 m) et le cimetière des
alpinistes

Rast auf dem Kleinglockner
(3783 m), den die berüchtigte
Glocknerscharte vom Großglockner
trennt

Resting on the Little Glockner
(12,412 ft), separated from the
Gross Glockner by the notorious
Glockner Fissure

Halte au sommet du Kleinglockner
(3783 m), sommet relié au
Grossglockner par une sorte de
crête, la «Glocknerscharte»

Eiszauber in der Riesen-Eishöhle
im Dachstein-Massiv

The magic of ice is seen in the
gigantic Ice Caves in the
Dachstein Massif

Féerie de la glace dans la grotte
glaciaire du massif du Dachstein

Der Hintere Gosausee mit dem
Hohen Dachstein (2996 m) über
dem Gosaugletscher

The Hinter Gosau Lake with the
Hohe Dachstein (9830 ft) above
the Gosau Glacier

«Hinterer Gosausee» et Hoher
Dachstein (2996 m) au-dessus
du glacier «Gosaugletscher» ▶

160 Das Große Wiesbachhorn (3571 m)   The Great Wiesbachhorn (11,716 ft)   Le Grand Wiesbachhorn (3571 m)
     vom Ferleitental aus gesehen   seen from Ferleitental   vu de la vallée de la Ferleiten

Im Friedhof von Heiligen-
blut erinnert ein Kreuz
und ein Gedenkbuch an
die im Glocknergebiet ver-
unglückten Bergsteiger;
im Hintergrund
der Großglockner

A cross in the Heiligenblut
Graveyard and an entry
in the Commemoration
Book are memorials to
the mountaineers who
perished in the Glockner
region; the Gross Glock-
ner in the background

Au cimetière de Heiligen-
blut, une croix et un livre
commémoratif rappellent
les alpinistes ayant trouvé
la mort dans le massif du
Glockner; à l'arrière-
plan, le Grossglockner

Hinterbichl im Virgental

Das 3436 m hohe Eiskögele
in der Glocknergruppe

Hinterbichl in the Virgen Valley

Eiskögele in the Glockner Group
is 11,267 ft high

Hinterbichl dans la vallée de la Virgen

Le Eiskögele, sommet du massif
du Glockner

163

Kerschbaumer Törl in den
Lienzer Dolomiten/Osttirol

Kerschbaum Törl in the Lienz
Dolomites (East Tyrol)

Le Kerschbaumer Törl dans les
Dolomites de Lienz (Tyrol Oriental)

Tiefblick zum Gesäuse genannten
Durchbruch der Enns durch die
Ennstaler Alpen

View into the "Gesäuse" where
the Enns breaks through the Enns
Valley Alps

De ce rocher, on domine le Gesäuse,
nom donné à la percée de l'Enns
dans le massif de la vallée de l'Enns

165

In ihren bizarren Formen gehören
die Vajolettürme in der
Rosengartengruppe und die Drei
Zinnen in den Sextener Dolomiten
(rechts) zu den markantesten
Gipfeln der Dolomiten

The most striking peaks in the
Dolomites are to be found among
these bizarre formations of the
Vajolettürme (towers) in the Rosengarten Group and the Drei Zinnen
in the Sexten Dolomites (right)

Les Vajolettürme, sommets du
Rosengarten, et les Drei Zinnen
(à droite), sommets du groupe de
la région de Sesto, sont des
sommets typiques des Dolomites

Großartig erheben sich die Geislerspitzen (3027 m) aus dem Villnösstal

The magnificient peaks of the Geisler
Spitzen soar up from the Villnöss
Valley to 9930 ft.

Les Geislerspitzen (3027 m) s'élèvent
majestueuses au-dessus de la
Villnösstal

Die Croda da Lago (2709 m) in
den Ampezzaner Dolomiten

Croda da Lago (8808 ft) in the
Ampezza Dolomites

La Croda da Lago (2709 m) dans
le massif d'Ampezzo

169

170   Frühling am Grödner Joch   Spring on the Grödner Joch   Impression printanière au Grödner Joch

Zu Füßen des Latemar (2794) liegt, märchengleich von Fichtenwäldern umgeben, der smaragdgrüne Karersee

As in a fairy-tale, the turquoise lake, Karersee, lies at the foot of Latemar (9167 ft), surrounded by fir woods

Le Karersee, lac au vert d'émeraude entouré de belles forêts de pins, s'étend au pied du Latemar (2794 m)

Skilift beim Grödner Joch, gegen
Große Tschierspitze (2592 m)

Ski lift near Grödner Joch,
towards the Great Tschier Spitze
(8504 ft)

Remonte-pente près du Grödner
Joch. A l'arrière-plan, la Grande
Tschierspitze (2592 m)

172

Mit ihrer vergletscherten
Nordflanke — einem idealen
Skigebiet — erhebt sich die
„Königin der Dolomiten" die
Marmolata (3344 m) über den
Fedaja-Stausee

Rising above the Fedaja Reservoir,
the Marmolata (10,965 ft), the
"Queen of the Dolomites", with
its glaciated North Flank and
ideal skiing slopes

La Marmolata (3344 m), la «reine
des Dolomites», se dresse
majestueuse au-dessus du lac
Fedaja. Le névé du versant nord
est pour les skieurs un véritable
paradis

173

Mächtig wuchtet der Monte Pelmo
(3168 m) aus dem Val Fiorentina empor

Monte Pelmo (10,394 ft) looms
hugely above the Val Fiorentina

Le Monte Pelmo (3168 m) domine
le val Fiorentina

Unter den Wänden der Sella-Gruppe
mit der Boé-Spitze (3151 m) führt
die Dolomitenstraße in zahlreichen
Windungen zum Sella-Joch

Below the rock faces of the Sella
Group with the Boé Spitze
(10,338 ft), the Dolomite Road leads
in numerous bends to Sella Joch

La route des Dolomites conduit en nombreux
lacets jusqu'au Sella-Joch; elle est dominée
par les parois abruptes du groupe de la Sella
dont la Boéspitze atteint 3151 mètres

An der Straße von Bozen nach
Venedig erhebt sich nach dem
Rolle-Paß eines der schönsten
Bergmassive der Dolomiten,
die bekannte Pala-Gruppe

One of the finest Dolomite massifs,
the well-known Pala Group, lifts its
head beyond the Rolle Pass on the
road from Bozen to Venice

Allant de Bolzano à Venise, on peut
admirer, après avoir passé le col de
Rolle, un des plus beaux massifs des
Dolomites, le groupe des Pala

Cimone della Pala, Rosetta, Pala di San Martino, Cima della Madonna und Sass Maor sind die klingenden Namen der gegen Himmel stürmenden Gipfel

Cimone della Pala, Rosetta, Pala di San Martino, Cima della Madonna and Sass Maor are the melodious names of these peaks jutting upwards into the heavens

Cimone della Pala, Rosetta, Pala di San Martino, Cima della Madonna et Sass Maor, tels sont les noms de ces sommets

Krokusblüte unter der Langkofel-
Gruppe: Grohmannspitze (3111 m),
Fünffingerspitze (2996 m),
178   Langkofel (3178 m)

Crocuses blooming below the Langkofel
Group: Grohmann Spitze (10,207 ft),
Fünffinger Spitze (9830 ft) and
Langkofel (10,427 ft)

Crocus en fleurs au pied du groupe
du Langkofel: Grohmannspitze
(3111 m), Fünffingerspitze (2996 m),
Langkofel (3178 m)

Der weltberühmte Wintersportplatz Cortina d'Ampezzo, am Fuße der gewaltigen Tofana (3243 m)

The world-famous winter-sports centre, Cortina d'Ampezzo at the foot of the mighty Tofana (10,639 ft)

Cortina d'Ampezzo, station de sports d'hiver célèbre dans le monde entier, est située au pied de l'imposante Tofana (3243 m)

179

180   Cadini-Gruppe (2839 m), nahe
Misurina, vom Westen gesehen

Cadini Group (9315 ft) near
Misurina, seen from the west

Le groupe du Cadini (2839 m),
près de Misurina, vu de l'ouest

Monte Cristallo (3216 m) und Piz
Popena (3152 m) von Tre Croci

Monte Cristallo (10,551 ft) and Piz
Popena (10,341 ft) seen from Tre Croci

Le Monte Cristallo (3216 m) et le
Piz Popena (3152 m) vus de Tre Croci   181

Der 2812 m hohe Sass Maor und
die Cima della Madonna (2733 m)
mit der Schleierkante, in der Pala
bei San Martino di Castrozza

Sass Maor (9226 ft) and Cima
della Madonna (8967 ft) with the
Schleierkante (Veil Edge) in the
Pala Dolomites near San Martino
di Castrozza

Le Sass Maor (2812 m) et la Cima
della Madonna (2733 m) ainsi que
la Schleierkante dans le groupe des
Pala près de San Martino di
Castrozza

Blick über das Cordévole-Tal zur
Civetta mit ihrer gewaltigen
Nordwest-Wand

View across the Cordévole Valley
towards Civetta with its colossal
North-West Face

La vallée de Cordévole et la
Civetta avec son imposante paroi
nord-ouest

183

Die eigenartige Felsgruppe der
Cinque Torri, der „Fünf Türme"

The unique group of crags resembling
five towers, the "Cinque Torri"

Une formation rocheuse pour le
moins bizarre, les Cinque Torri

Brentei-Hütte und Crozzon di
Brenta (3135 m) mit seiner 1000 m
hohen Nordkante

Brentei Hut and Crozzon di
Brenta (10,286 ft) with its 3281-ft
North Edge

Le refuge de Brentei et le Crozzon
di Brenta (3135 m) avec son arête
haute de 1000 mètres

185

Die Brenta gehört zwar zu den
Nonsberger Alpen, gleicht aber in
ihrem Charakter den Dolomiten.
Von der Malga Ritorta offenbart sie
sich in Ehrfurcht gebietender Größe

Though the Brenta belongs to the
Nonsberg Alps, in its character it
resembles the Dolomites more.
Towards the Malga Ritorta,
its awesome grandeur is revealed

La Brenta appartient au massif des
Nonsberger mais ressemble
beaucoup aux Dolomites. Vue de
la Malga Ritorta, elle apparaît
dans toute sa magnificence

Im Kletterparadies der Dolomiten.
Abseilen vom Campanile Brabante
in der Civetta-Gruppe

In the cragsman's paradise of the Dolomites. Roping down from the Campanile Brabante in the Civetta Group

Les Dolomites, eldorado des alpinistes.
Descente en rappel au Campanile
Brabante dans le massif de la Civetta

Felsgebilde von seltener Schönheit: Torre di Brenta (3014 m), Campanile Basso (Guglia di Brenta; 2877 m) und Cima Brenta Alta (2966 m)

Rock formations of rare beauty: Torre di Brenta (9889 ft), Guglia di Brenta (9439 ft) and Cima Brenta Alta (9830 ft)

Formations rocheuses d'une rare beauté: Torre di Brenta (3014 m), Guglia di Brenta (2877 m) et Cima Brenta Alta (2966 m)

Bocca di Brenta (2552 m) und
Cima Brenta (3150 m)

Bocca di Brenta (8373 ft) and
Cima Brenta (10,335 ft)

Bocca di Brenta (2552 m) et Cima
Brenta (3150 m)

Vielgestaltig und kontrastreich, kühne Felstürme und von den Naturgewalten zernagte Wände: das ist die Brenta-Gruppe. Hier vom Monte Spinale gesehen

Multiform and rich in contrasts, hazardous rocky pinnacles and eroded rock faces: that is the Brenta Group. Here is a view of it from Monte Spinale

Variété et contrastes, tours rocheuses aux formes téméraires et parois rongées par l'érosion, telles sont les caractéristiques du massif de la Brenta. Vue prise du Monte Spinale

191

Die imposante Gardesana
Occidentale am Westufer
des Gardasees (1931)

The imposing "Gardesana
Occidentale" on the west
shore of Lake Garda
(1931)

L'imposante Gardesana
Occidentale sur la rive
ouest du Lac de Garde
a été aménagée en 1931

Ein einsamer Wächter,
mit bis zu 200 m hohen
Felsabstürzen, der Cam-
panile di Val Montanaia
(2171 m) in den Karni-
schen Alpen

A solitary sentinel with
rocky precipices dropping
over 650 ft, the Campa-
nile di Val Montanaia
(7123 ft) in the Carnic
Alps

Le Campanile di Val
Montanaia (2171 m) dont
les parois verticales
atteignent jusqu'à 200
mètres ressemble à une
sentinelle solitaire veillant
sur les alentours

Karnische Alpen — Blick nordwestlich vom Rifugio Pordenone (1205 m)

The Carnic Alps; the north-west scene from Rifugio Pordenone (3953 ft)

Dans les Alpes Carniques. Vue prise du Rifugio Pordenone (1205 m) vers le nord-ouest

194

Blick vom Monte S. Simeon in das
Tagliamento-Tal bei Venzone

Scene in the Tagliamento Valley
near Venzone, from Monte
S. Simeon

Du Monte S. Simeon, le regard
plonge dans le Val Tagliamento
près de Venzone

Bled, bekannter slowenischer Kurort, zwischen den Julischen Alpen und den Karawanken gelegen

The well-known Slovene health resort, Bled, lies between the Julian Alps and the Karawanken Range

Bled, localité pittoresque de Slovénie, est située entre les Alpes Juliennes et le massif des Karawanken

Bohinj, in den Julischen Alpen, am Wocheiner See, mit beachtenswerter Kirche aus dem 14. Jahrhundert

Bohinj on the Wochein Lake in the Julian Alps has a noteworthy church dating from the 14th century

Bohinj, ville des Alpes Juliennes située sur le lac du même nom, possède une église intéressante construite au 14e siècle

197

Von den höchsten Gipfeln der
Julischen Alpen umgeben liegt
Kranjska Gora im Dreiländereck
in der Oberkrain

Surrounded by the highest peaks
of the Julian Alps, Kranjska Gora
is situated in a corner where three
countries meet, in the Upper Krain

Kranjska Gora se trouve dans
l'Oberkrain, entourée des
principaux sommets des Alpes
Juliennes

Cäsar gab der herrlichen Bergwelt
der Julischen Alpen seinen Namen.
Ein Paradies für Bergwanderer

Caesar gave his own name to this
magnificent range of the Alps.
A paradise for mountain-climbers

César a donné son nom — Alpes
Juliennes — à ce magnifique
paysage alpestre, un paradis pour
l'amateur d'excursions en montagne

Ob im Sommer oder im Winter,
die mächtige Schönheit der Julischen
Alpen zwingt zur Bewunderung

In summer as in winter, the majestic
beauty of the Julian Alps compels
one's admiration

Les Alpes Juliennes conservent
toujours leur beauté majestueuse,
que ce soit en hiver ou en été

Save-Quelle mit Mojstrovka
(2323 m) und Jalovec (2643 m)

The source of the Save with
Mojstrovka (7622 ft) and Jalovec
(8671 ft)

Source de la Save. A l'arrière-plan,
Mojstrovka (2323 m) et Jalovec
(2643 m)

Zur Freude der Eingeweihten noch viel zu wenig bekannt ...

Still too little known—to the joy of the initiated ...

Encore très peu connue à la grande joie des initiés ...

202

... das ideale und weiträumige Skigebiet um den Komna (1520 m)

... the extensive and ideal skiing grounds round the Komna, 1520 m (4987 ft)

... une région idéale pour les skieurs, autour du Komna (1520 m)

Blick vom Vrata-Tal zum Triglav
(2863 m), dem höchsten Gipfel der
Julischen Alpen

View from the Vrata Valley
towards Triglav (9396 ft), the
highest peak in the Julian Alps

Le Triglav (2863 m), point
culminant des Alpes Juliennes,
vu de la vallée de Vrata

An der Skrlatica (2738 m) vorbei
führt die Straße über den Vršič-
Sattel (Werschetz-Sattel — 1611 m)
in das Trenta-Tal

The road over the Werschetz
(Vršič) Saddle (5286 ft) into the
Trenta Valley skirts the Skrlatica
(8983 ft)

Longeant la Skrlatica (2738 m),
la route passant au col de Vršič
(1611 m) descend vers la vallée de
Trenta

Im Gebiet der Kamniški Alpen (Steiner Alpen). Die Flugschanze von Planica

In the Kamniški Alps (Steiner Alps). The Planica long-distance ski-jumping hill (for ski-flying)

Dans les Kamniški Alpes (Steiner Alpen). Le grand tremplin de saut à skis de Planica

Bildbände im Verlag Ludwig Simon

Überraschend vielseitig und dabei erstaunlich preiswert!

Bisher sind erschienen:

Ägypten	Holland	Schweden
Bayern	Italien	Schweiz
Deutschland	Jugoslawien	Skandinavien
Frankreich	Österreich	Spanien
Griechenland	Portugal	

Bundesrepublik Deutschland

Ein Bildband im Großformat, 270 Seiten, davon 100 mit Farbbildern und 100 mit Schwarzweiß-Aufnahmen. Text und Bildunterschriften in deutsch, englisch und französisch.

Luftbilder aus der DDR

Ein Bildband im Großformat, 168 Text- und Bildseiten, mit 60 Farbbildern und über 100 Schwarzweiß-Aufnahmen, die 1968 exklusiv für diesen Band erflogen wurden.

Die Alpen

Ein Bildband im Großformat, mit Aufnahmen aus den Alpen Frankreichs, der Schweiz, Deutschlands, Österreichs, Italiens und Jugoslawiens. 210 Seiten, davon 40 mit Farbbildern und 130 mit Schwarzweiß-Aufnahmen. Text und Bildunterschriften in deutsch, englisch und französisch.

Allgäu	Harz	Am Rhein entlang
Baden	Hessen	Rheinland-Pfalz
Bayer. Königsschlösser	München	Schleswig-Holstein
Berner Oberland	Niedersachsen	Schwarzwald
Dolomiten	Nordrhein	Vierwaldstätter See
Engadin	Oberammergau	Wallis
Frankenland	Oberbayern	Westfalen
Genfer See	Potsdam	Wien
		Württemberg

Weitere Bände sind in Vorbereitung!

Verlag Ludwig Simon · München-Pullach